P9-BIK-701

THE *Non* CYCLIST'S GUIDE TO THE CENTURY

AND OTHER ROAD RACES

GET ON YOUR BUTT AND INTO GEAR

Dawn Dais

SEAL PRESS

The Noncyclist's Guide to the Century and Other Road Races
Get On Your Butt and Into Gear
Copyright © 2009 by Dawn Dais

Published by
Seal Press
A Member of Perseus Books Group
1700 Fourth Street
Berkeley, California

All rights reserved. No part of this book may be reproduced or transmitted in any form without written permission from the publisher, except by reviewers who may quote brief excerpts in connection with a review.

Library of Congress Cataloging-in-Publication Data

Dais, Dawn.
  The noncyclist's guide to the century and other road races : get on your
butt and into gear / Dawn Dais.
      p. cm.
  ISBN-13: 978-1-58005-268-9
  ISBN-10: 1-58005-268-1
  1. Bicycle racing. I. Title.
  GV1049.D33 2009
  796.6'2--dc22
                                    2008051979

Cover design by Tabitha Lahr
Interior design by Megan Cooney
Printed in the United States of America
Distributed by Publishers Group West

TABLE of CONTENTS

INTRODUCTION   1

CHAPTER *one*   THE BIKE   5

CHAPTER *two*   THE TRAINING   63

CHAPTER *three*   THE RIDING   129

CHAPTER *four*   THE BIG EVENT   211

EPILOGUE   246

APPENDIX *A*   ACCESSORY CHECKLIST   249

APPENDIX *B*   CENTURY CHECKLIST   253

APPENDIX *C*   TRAINING LOG   257

Introduction

So here we go again. My last book, *The NonRunner's Marathon Guide for Women,* shared my harrowing tale of marathon training (and crying), as well as a plethora of information on how people might begin their own journey to a marathon finish line (crying tips included). After hearing from readers throughout the land about how my little book inspired them to finish their first marathon, or to tackle the sport of running, I couldn't help but be inspired myself. Maybe it was time for me to put myself out there again, to test my body, mind, and soul with a physical challenge that at first glance seemed altogether horrific. Ahhh, isn't personal enrichment great?

As I searched to find the perfect challenge for my weary body, cycling repeatedly came up as a good option. It had all the pain and sweat running did, but without the high impact. This was great news for my knees, which were still a bit battered from my foray into pavement pounding. I was also intrigued when I discovered that cyclists are supposed to wear helmets. This led me to the conclusion that cycling would have me moving so fast that my brain matter would actually be put at risk. This sounded like an exciting addition to my normal athletic endeavors. Someone once recommended that I wear a helmet while training for a marathon, but that had less to do with my speed and more to do with my repeatedly banging my head against the trees along the running trail out of general frustration with the sport. However, in cycling the helmet is there to protect you *during* the sport, not as a result of your angry outbursts *in response* to the sport. Fantastic.

Having gathered these exciting facts, I decided to make cycling the next lucky recipient of my general disdain and bad attitude. Lance Armstrong rejoiced. Finally, his sport would get a little attention.

You would think a sport in which I am actually required to wear butt-padded shorts, because of the amount of sitting involved, would be just the sort of sport I've been looking for. But then you might be forgetting about all of that pesky pedaling. And about the fact that the shorts, like those found in the sport of running, are once again made of spandex.

And yet still I persevered, for the sake of others like me, into a foreign land full of the physically fit and steel-thighed. I braved the harsh terrain and harsher crotch rashes so that I might come back and tell the tale of how one gets off her butt and tackles the world of cycling. Though this particular tale actually starts with getting back on your butt by sitting down on a bike.

See? It's not all bad. And guess what? There are wheels involved, too. (Blessed be the word "coasting.")

Once I pedaled into the world of cycling, I was shocked to find out there was more to it than merely cussing on two wheels (sometimes the cussing would continue after I got *off* the bike, too). All sorts of people use their bikes for all sorts of activities. Some trained for two-hundred-mile races, some rode to work, some traveled the world, and some just spent leisurely summer nights cruising around their neighborhoods. Yet, as different as their goals, or even their approach to the sport, may have been, all of these people were cyclists. And once you hop on your bike, you'll be a cyclist, too—and I'd like to help you figure out what kind you'd like to be.

Whether you are looking to tackle a long-distance event or are just looking to incorporate a little more exercise into your daily life, cycling offers all sorts of options. My hope with this book is to make you aware of all those options and help you decide which ones might be a good fit for you and your lifestyle.

If you are looking for a big challenge, a hundred-mile century ride might be just crazy enough to inspire your interest. A century is sorta the marathon of cycling, if marathons lasted twelve hours instead of six, and if afterward you iced your aching butt instead of your aching knees. One hundred miles is an admirable and challenging goal for new and experienced cyclists alike. For those of you looking to be admired and challenged, I've employed the aid of a cycling professional to write a training schedule (see Chapter 2) that will prepare you for your first one-hundred-mile adventure.

If one hundred miles seem like a little too much for you to tackle right now, there are still many ways for you to set a cycling goal and achieve it. (Some of these goals involve booze and/or donuts, so you might have just found your favorite sport.) As you flip through the pages of this book, you'll find tips and info aplenty about how to purchase, ride, and maximize your bike. (You might want to skip straight to the page about donuts—why even bother with the rest?) But as with anything you take on, the real meat of cycling is found in the journey: the people you meet along the way, the detours you take, the restaurants you discover.

As much as I hated to admit it, I actually found cycling quite an adventure—one that took me through the Swiss Alps, over the Brooklyn Bridge, and down streets of my hometown that I'd never actually traveled in all the years I'd lived there. Of course, the adventure also took me to the masseuse for a full-body massage, to the side of the road with a number of flat tires, and over my handlebars onto a not-so-welcoming sidewalk. Adventures aren't all sunshine and poppy fields, is my point.

If you're ready for a little fun, a lot of challenge, and a sprinkling of butt numbness, turn the page and let's get this ride started.

CHAPTER *one*

The Bike

The most important thing you are going to need when deciding to tackle the sport of cycling (besides quite a bit of delusion and an affinity for butt soreness) is the actual bike. If you're like me, you might be a little intimidated by the many options you'll have when it comes to buying a bike. Also, if you're like me, you may deal with this intimidation by simply walking into the first bike store you see and saying, "I need a bike!" without first doing even a smidgen of research. Don't be like me. It could end poorly. As it turns out, finding a bike that fits you is slightly more important than whether or not the bike has cool pink flower designs on it. Who knew?

THE PREP

Bikes do not come cheap, so it really is in your best interest to put a little thought into exactly what kind of bike would be best for you. Basically, there are two ways you can go about finding the right bike for you—well, three if you count my patented Walk into a Bike Shop and Ask for a Bike method. But we'll go over the two that are actually legitimately good bike-purchasing methods. The first involves a lot of work, and the other, not so much. While I'm usually a big fan of anything that involves not so much work, there is something to be said for the time-intensive plan as well. In part because the more time you spend *finding* your bike, the more time you can spend *not riding* your bike. Which is a great way to start your training program, if you ask me.

Both of your buying options are going to require you to first have some basic information about yourself, which will help you figure out what bike will work best for you.

Basic Information

WHERE ARE YOU GOING TO RIDE?

This question refers mostly to terrain. Where are you going to be doing most of your cycling? Will you be riding on roads, on off-road dirt trails, or perhaps both? This question will be the deciding factor in what type of bike you end up getting.

WHY ARE YOU GOING TO RIDE?

What is the main goal you hope to accomplish after taking on the cycling world (besides being able to add the words "butt butter" to your vocabulary)? Are you wanting to have an alternate form of transportation around your neighborhood? Do you want to do a charity event? Do you want to get back in shape? Do you want to do a century ride? Do you hope to bring handlebar streamers back into mainstream cycling? It's important to know your goals so that you get a bike that will help you accomplish them.

HOW MUCH DO YOU WANT TO SPEND?

Be realistic about this one. I know it's exciting to jump on the Yay, a New Sport! bandwagon and convince yourself that you must buy the absolute best products and accessories, or else your bandwagon will become a sadwagon full of unattained cycling hopes and dreams. That doesn't necessarily have to be the case. Top-of-the-line bikes can end up costing you thousands of dollars, and that is a lot of money to drop on what may turn out to be a short-lived foray into cycling. Bikes can range in price from $700 to $4,000, with all sorts of options in between. Get a price range in your head that sounds doable for you and then begin looking at what kinds of bikes are available in that price range.

Do not feel like you have to get a top-of-the-line bike in order to live out your cycling dreams. Unless you are a supercyclist, it is most likely that you aren't going to be able to notice an extreme difference between a bike made out of space-age materials and one made out of earthbound products. The most important thing for a new cyclist is to get a bike that fits her the best, and that bike is not always going to be the most expensive one available.

Also keep in mind that unless you plan on riding the bike naked (and there are actual races that encourage that, so that's a possibility), you are also going to be dropping at least another few hundred dollars on clothes and accessories and ice packs (if you do ride naked, you are going to need more than a few ice packs).

WHAT LEVEL OF CYCLIST ARE YOU?

Methinks if you picked up a book with the word "NonCyclist" in the title, you might not be in training for the next Tour de France, which is fine, 'cause who can afford all the drugs required for that race? This question is just asking you to take note of your physical prowess (or lack thereof). This will help you pick a bike that is made for someone of your particular level of fitness (sorry, no motors or engines allowed).

WHAT LEVEL OF CYCLIST DO YOU WANT TO BE?

Are you going into this new sport with the hope of one day becoming a supercyclist who throws away her car keys and travels the world by bike? Or are you thinking that it would be great if you could just stick with this newfound hobby long enough to actually get the bike out of the garage at some point? Or are you somewhere in between, someone who'd like to start up a regular cycling schedule and stick with it in order to stay healthy and have some fun? The point of this question is to find out if you are going to outgrow the limitations of your bike in the near future. If you are, then it might be a good idea to buy a little bit nicer bike now so that you don't have to buy a completely new bike once you transform into a cycling machine and begin tackling double century rides on a weekly basis. (This is where those Tour de France drugs would come in handy.)

Now that you've taken the time to consider some of your goals, you are ready to go out in search of The Bike.

Bike Buying Plan #1

Go online, consult books, read magazines, and figure out not only what kind of bike you want but what brand you want as well. Read online reviews, take notes, and narrow your search down to one or two bikes that will most closely fit your needs (a moped probably shouldn't be on that list, just FYI). The Internet is a fantastic place—and not just because of that Daily Puppy website and the fact that you can find Milli Vanilli music videos on YouTube. There are also forums galore where you can go and pick the brains of other cycling enthusiasts, and read their opinions on all things bike. If you give them some of your General Information (no social security numbers, please), they will probably be able to give you some advice on what bike they would recommend. As with anything on the Internet, get more than one opinion before making your choice. But just like puppies and Milli Vanilli videos, opinions on bikes are plentiful on the Internet, so you should have no problem seeking them out.

Bike Info on the Superhighway

- www.bicycling.com/gear

- www.bikeforums.net

- http://forums.teamestrogen.com

- http://forums.roadbikereview.com

This Bike Buying Plan will be a *ton* of fun for some people. In fact, researching a new hobby is the best part for some people. They are all about doing due diligence and can't get enough of online investigating. These people generally own several different colored highlighters and most likely a subscription to *Consumer Reports*. The technical name for these people is "dorks," but I guess you can also find them filed under the words "smart" or "intelligent."

I myself have never been accused of being smart (although my dance moves do qualify me for the dork title), and have actually been known to walk impulsively onto a car lot and proclaim, "I want a red one." So, needless to say, I didn't pick Bike Buying Plan #1. Did my bike work out okay? Yes. Did I get the very best bike for me? I have no idea, though I honestly wish I could answer yes.

Bike Buying Plan #2

Fill out the My General Information questionnaire on page 24 with as many details as you can. Then tear it out, pin it to yourself, and head in the general direction of a cycle shop. Hopefully, as if you were a poor abandoned child, someone will eventually come to your aid, read your General Information, and give you a bike in exchange for the wad of cash you have in your hand. When this happens, see if they'll throw in a water bottle.

In addition to your General Information and Bike Buying Plan, you should have at least a little bit of an idea about what sorts of bikes are out there vying for your attention. Below I've outlined some different types of bikes you'll find at the cycle shops. Most likely, you are going to end up with a road bike, but it's good to know what else is out there so you can sound knowledgeable during all the upcoming conversations about bikes that you are inevitably going to get into once you start actually riding a bike. Also, just because you are riding a boring road bike doesn't mean you should be uninformed about the other cool bikes that are out there. And by "cool" I mean reclinable. Yeah, I'm not kidding. They're awesome.

Bike Type

ROAD RACER

These bikes are like the Cadillac of road bikes—in that they are the top of the line, not in that they are bulky and big. In fact, these bikes are the opposite. They are slick and smooth and made for going fast. These are probably much more bike than a non-cyclist really needs. The reality is that you will probably be more comfortable on a less snazzy bike, because these bikes are made for the skills and handling abilities of professionals, and you might be just slightly below that level. Which is good, because these bikes cost at least $4,000. And anything that costs that much should have four wheels, or have the words "wall-size" and "plasma" in its name.

ROAD SPORT

If you are training with the intent of doing a road race or century ride, you will most likely be purchasing a bike in this category. These bikes are built to be light and fast, but also comfortable and durable. Their frames are made out of light materials, and they have "drop" handlebars. "Drop" is a fancy word for rounded handlebars that drop down on the sides, below the normal handlebars, offering you another, lower place to put your hands while you are riding. "Drop" is also an appropriate word because you have to drop your upper body down to put your hands on these handlebars. Unfortunately, the word does not apply to your ass in this riding scenario. I'm sure this positioning has to do with aerodynamics or some such science, but all I know is, these bikes force to me to engage in a sport where my butt is nearly higher than my head for most of the activity. It's not a look I've ever gotten comfortable with.

Road sport bikes also have many gears, which will help you with the pesky hills that never fail to show up when people are engaging in outdoor athletic activities. Trust me when I say you will come to love your low gears in ways you never knew you could feel for inanimate objects. Do not feel bad that these gears are usually referred to as "granny gears," perhaps because only a granny should require such easy pedaling. As someone who has been *passed* my many an older woman, I must say that I'm actually disappointed the gears don't make me go as fast as the grannies.

The only downside to these bikes, I've found, is their small tires. The skinny tires are meant to combine with the light weight and your hunched-over position to make you into a human bullet of sorts, cutting through the air with precision and speed. This speed tends to decrease slightly, however, when said skinny tires explode because you ran over a pebble. It's at that point that your bullet loses some of its oomph.

I had issues with the tires on my road bikes, but I also have issues with all tires. It's sorta my thing. Some people knit, I get flat tires. We all have to be good at something. But I've talked to people who have normal relationships with tires. Some have never gotten flats on their road bikes, and others eventually switched to a hybrid because they got so tired of fixing flats out on the road. I think it's a crapshoot as to what you will experience, but it's worth it to be aware that flats are a very real possibility with road bikes.

There are a few options out there as far as road bike tires go. I had my Bike Maintenance Dude put some special lining stuff inside my tires, in hopes of stopping all puncturing objects. There are also slightly heavier, more durable tires you can put on your bike that might stay unflat for longer. The people I've talked to who got these tires were happy with their choice. You do end up losing a little in speed when you go with a heavier tire, but the fact that the tires stay inflated better is a fair trade for many cyclists.

These bikes range in price, from $700 up to $2,000 or more, so do your research on what brand or model looks best to you and is closest to your budget.

TOURING

Touring bikes still fall into the road bike category, but are made for a slightly different purpose than simple road races. These bikes are designed for people who are interested in, you guessed it, touring with their bikes. Not as in, "I'll be here all week! Tip your wait-staff!" sort of touring, but more along the lines of "Have bike, will travel." I'll go into greater detail about bike touring in Chapter 3, but these bikes are generally made for those who feel like packing some stuff, throwing it on a bike, and going out to see the world. I know, I know, there are Winnebagos for that kind of thing, but honestly, seeing the world from a bike is one of the coolest things you'll ever have the opportunity to do, and this bike can help you do it a little more easily.

I actually did some bike touring, but I did it on a regular road sport bike. It was a great experience, but if I were considering making bike tourism a regular activity of mine, I would definitely consider getting one of these bikes. They are more durable than other road bikes, with fatter tires and special mounts where you can throw your loaded packs (or hitchhikers, if you feel so inclined). Their handlebars allow for a more upright cycling position, which many people may appreciate on longer, world-traveling rides.

The only drawback to these bikes is their additional weight, but in the end durability is worth the added weight. Because when you are heading out to the middle of the Swiss Alps, it's nice to know that you are on a reliable bike that won't require you to catch a cow back to the hotel at some point.

HYBRID

A hybrid bike is basically a hybrid of a road bike and a mountain bike. Some people really like these bikes because they allow the rider the option of riding on varying terrain. And variety is supposedly the spice of life. But in reality these bikes aren't really spicy so much as they are sorta bland. They aren't really great road bikes and they aren't really great mountain bikes. They're good if you are interested in riding casually both on- and off-road, and many cyclists absolutely love their hybrid. But if you're serious about either on- or off-road cycling, you should just commit to the bike made specifically for your terrain of choice.

MOUNTAIN BIKE

Mountain bikes are designed for the, um, mountain, in that they are made for off-road riding. Their tires are fatter and tougher, so they can take on rough terrain. The handlebars are higher and straight, which allows you to sit upright while riding and also allows you more control over the bike, which you'll need when riding over bumpy surfaces.

Many cyclists use their mountain bikes for places other than the mountain. They prefer the design and durability of the bike and choose to ride it both on- and off-road. Mountain bikes can be good commuter or everyday bikes because they allow for a more comfortable (not completely bent over) ride, and are a little better equipped to take on the uneven, bumpy streets you may find on your way to work.

These are great bikes if your main cycling goal is to do mostly off-road riding, or perhaps if you are just looking to ditch the car and become a hip bike commuter. But if you are hoping to do long road races, you are going to find that a mountain bike just isn't as fast or as well suited to that particular kind of riding.

RECUMBENT

"Recumbent" is another word for "recline," which itself is another word for "awesome." These bikes are the ones you see cruising by you low to the ground with the rider actually lying back against a backrest. *A backrest!* His feet are out in front of him, pedaling while he basically naps. I've been known to yell at these men when they go by, "That guy has a *pillow!* I want a pillow!" I seriously think I could get excited about a sport that involved my lying down the entire time. I'm sure these cyclists are exerting some effort with the whole pedaling thing, but good lord, this is like pedaling in their recliner. If I could get a flat-screen on one of those bad boys, I'd be winning Tour de Everyplaces each weekend. *And* I'd be all caught up on my TiVo. It's all about multitasking.

People who enjoy these bikes ride them just like any other road bike, on both flat and hilly routes. I imagine this would take some getting used to, because I can't really figure out how they get up steep hills without the help of a towing company. The way they have to be pedaled makes me think my thigh muscles would have to be considerably larger in order for me to make it over even a speed bump on this bike. But the good news is, you'd totally have someplace to nap while you were getting your energy up for the climb. . . .

UTILITY

These bikes are commonly referred to as cruisers. I also like to refer to them as Pimp Daddies—not be confused with P. Diddy. Although I don't doubt that P. would love him a cruiser bike. Cruisers are definitely very high on my list of top bikes because 1) they can be purchased with banana seats and streamers, and 2) about 83 percent of the time, the riders of these bikes are drinking some sort of beverage while cruising around town. They've got one hand on their handlebars (the stupidly high ones that are almost above their head) and the other around a large tasty beverage. Now, I'm not implying that cruiser riders enjoy a cocktail, but I will note that these bikes have become very popular among fans of bar crawls. I'm pretty sure it's not altogether legal or even that smart to combine these (or any moving object) with the consumption of alcohol, but I can't say that it's never crossed my mind that extreme intoxication might be the only way I would truly enjoy any sport.

These bikes aren't made exclusively for the transportation of lushes, though; they are also quite a bit of fun for jetting around town or heading out for a leisurely afternoon ride. The key thing to remember about these bikes is the word "leisurely." Nothing fast is happening on these bikes (which is good, 'cause then you might spill your beverage), but they will get you where you are going and they will get you there looking like a Pimp Daddy. Top that, Armstrong.

The Purchase

With your General Information, Bike Buying Plan, and knowledge of the different bike types, you are all set to head out to your local cycle shop and make your purchase. Here are some tips to help you with this final step.

Befriend Cyclists

One of the greatest things I've discovered when foraying into new sports (in addition to several not-so-great things, a couple of which involved rashes) is that the people hanging out in those sports are always really cool, and more than willing to help you out. You have to figure that if these adults are choosing to spend their precious time doing any sport, they must enjoy it. They also must be a little kooky, which is a great combination when you are looking for information. Kooky people who really enjoy things are always more than happy to tell you all about their hobby of choice. Frankly, they are sorta waiting for someone to ask them about it, because they are teeming with helpful hints, just ready to be unleashed on an uninformed coach potato.

Most likely, you already know a cyclist or two (they're the ones on the bikes), but if you don't, there's no shortage of online forums and cycling groups. Befriend these people and have them bestow their knowledge upon you. The best knowledge they can bestow is probably their choice of cycle shops. They probably have one or two shops they frequent where the people are nice and the merchandise is good. This information alone will help you immensely (but probably not as much as if they just let you ride on their handlebars for your whole road race).

Picking a Cycle Shop

The most important decision you'll make when buying your bike is where you buy it. If you pick a good place with honest, knowledgeable Bike People, you are going to be fine. These people will spend a good deal of time with you, helping you decide exactly what bike is right for you. They will have handy machines that will measure your body and spit out numbers and tell the Bike People the correct setup for your bike. (Don't worry, the machine can't tell that you're out of shape. Or at least it won't tell anyone else . . .) In addition, they will have Bike Mechanic Guys who can help you throughout your training with anything that seems to be going wrong with your bike. I once had to actually take my bike into my cycle shop and ask them how to change the gears. And the Bike Dude didn't even snicker when he showed me. That's a sign of a good person, if you ask me.

Picking the right cycle shop will also ease your fears that you might be taken advantage of because you are a newbie with a credit card. I'd recommend talking to local cyclists and going online to read customer reviews before you pick a shop. Overall, I've had good luck with the salespeople in bike shops. They are always cyclists themselves and therefore encyclopedias of information on their sport. They are usually super-laid-back people with great personalities who are ready and willing to answer even the stupidest questions (note my "How do I change the gears on this bike?" example above).

And it's generally in their best interest to treat you well and not try to sell you on something that isn't right for you. If you are there shelling out cash for a new bike, you are mostly likely jumping headfirst into a new sport. And anyone who is jumping headfirst into a new sport is most likely not going to stop at a new bike. They're also going to need all the accessories and clothes and snacks. Which means they are going to be returning to the cycle shop quite frequently, following each ride, when they realize they are missing things they need. (Unfortunately, the shops don't sell powerful leg muscles. I've looked several times.)

If you are out on a ride and a fellow cyclist tells you that you paid too much for your bike, or you got the wrong bike for your needs, then you aren't going to return to your cycle shop, so they've lost a great repeat customer. On the other hand, if they treat you well, you're likely to tell others to visit their shop, and then they've gained even more return customers. I'm pretty sure this is all Business 101, but it's still a good thing to remember when you are timidly entering a store full of bikes that cost more than your mortgage payment.

When you go into a cycle shop, be prepared to actually test out the merchandise before you make your purchase. When I was training for a marathon, I was made to run in the shoe store before I bought my running shoes; similarly, when I bought my bike I rode it around the parking lot before I made my decision (though it would have taken a lot to change my mind about the cool pink flower-painted one). It's more of a nice gesture, I figure, since you probably find that most problems arise well past the five-minute mark. I myself am an exception to the rule, however, since I generally start having issues almost immediately after even thinking about engaging in athletic activities. But not everyone can be at my level of athleticism.

Test-Drive

Buying a bike and pedaling into the cycling world is a big decision. Unlike in most other sports, it's very difficult to casually test out cycling without making a pretty large investment. It would be like thinking about taking up soccer when the ball cost $1,000 and you still had to buy shoes, too. That's quite a financial commitment to make to something that you don't even know you like. It would be like having a wedding before you'd even met the person. It could turn out badly. And either way, you could end up with a pain in the ass.

One way to avoid jumping blindly into bike buying is to try out the sport before you make your purchase. You can do this by finding a bike, hopping on it, and riding around for a while. (Try to make sure the owner of said bike is in on your plan.) And not just a little while—maybe find a friend who is a cyclist already and plan a riding excursion with that person. Nothing too crazy, though, 'cause you don't want to completely terrify yourself right off the bat. Complete terror isn't scheduled until week three of your training, usually.

Borrow a bike from a friend or rent a bike from a local shop for a few hours. If you go to a good shop, they will fit the bike to you and you'll have a pretty good idea of how you are going to feel about cycling by the end of your trial run. The only thing to be cautious of is the fact that you are probably going to be in pain, so don't let that be the only thing that deters you from the sport. I mean, if we were going to start eliminating athletic activities because of pain, all we'd be left with would be that supercompetitive chess that old men play in city parks. And even that looks like it could hurt your hand after the tenth time you slam that clock on the side of the table.

My point is, your trial ride on the bike isn't really to see if you are comfortable with cycling, or even that good at it. Those things will come in time. The point is to go out on a pretty bike path with a friend, chitchat about life and your sore butt, and get a feel for what it means to hop on a bike and go for a ride. It might sound silly, but some people just don't enjoy cycling. Maybe it's not their thing. Maybe they've never heard of the reclining bikes. And just because you and your childhood BFF used to *love* riding bikes down to the 7-Eleven twenty years ago doesn't mean you are going to *love* long-distance cycling (although it might help if you figure out a way to work the 7-Eleven into your road races— I'm just sayin').

Most likely, you will have a good time on your test-drive and realize that you have long been suppressing your inner Armstrong. When this happens, you can feel confident that dropping a large sum on this new sport is worth it. It might even eliminate some of the hesitation you feel about making such a large purchase. I mean, it's clear you are going to be a cycling machine, so your endorsement deals will more than cover the cost of the bike within a month or two, right? Right.

Show Me What You're Working With

In addition to style, bikes vary in material. Supercyclists can talk at great length about all of these materials and their pros and cons. It might be something worth bringing up at about mile 72, when you really need something to get your mind off things for the next hour or so. Until then, here is a brief breakdown of the wonders that are bike materials.

STEEL
Old-school
Sturdy
Heavy
Found on cheaper bikes
Tendency to rust

ALUMINUM
Lighter than steel
Not that expensive
Doesn't absorb shocks so well

TITANIUM
Lightweight
Durable
Smooth ride
Expensive

CARBON FIBER
NASA-type material
Superlight
Absorbs bumps well
Expensive
Not so durable (which is probably much worse news for NASA than for you)

My General Information

Jot down your answers to the following General Information questions, and photocopy or take this page with you when you go to purchase your bike. This will help the Bike Dude figure out what bike will work best for you, and will probably end up saving you a lot of trial-and-error time in the store. Well, at least some of the trial time, as I'd venture to say the error stuff is unavoidable when starting a new sport.

WHERE ARE YOU GOING TO RIDE?

WHY ARE YOU GOING TO RIDE?

HOW MUCH DO YOU WANT TO SPEND?

WHAT LEVEL OF CYCLIST ARE YOU?

WHAT LEVEL OF CYCLIST DO YOU WANT TO BE?

Pimping Your Bike

So you've done a bunch of research—gone to a few stores, tried out ten bikes—and you've finally made your decision! You've found the perfect bike for you! You are ready to make your purchase and ride off into the sunset. But before you can get to the horizon, or even the checkout counter, you notice how many other things there are for sale in this store. And then you notice an inexplicable impulse to buy each and every one of these items.

As it turns out, getting out of the cycle shop without buying three hundred accessories is actually the first endurance test of your training schedule. You might even want to carb up for it, 'cause you are going to need as much strength as you can get.

The key to accessory purchasing is to start small. You can slowly work your way up to owning an entire catalog's worth of bicycle whatnots, but there's no need to rush right into it. This isn't like packing for a vacation overseas, when you feel the need to fill your suitcase with everything you could possibly need on your trip. ("A cold front might come through the Bahamas; I should pack this parka just in case.") Don't go with the "better safe than sorry" method of accessory purchasing right off the bat.

It's tempting when starting a new sport to load up on everything in sight, in hopes of buying your way to success. But the fact is, you don't need to buy every single gadget and knickknack in order to be successful. Some very good cyclists are minimalists where their accessories are concerned, while others can't get enough of the extras. There's no way to tell where you fall on that spectrum until you hit the road and figure out what kind of cyclist you really are—and it will be quite a bummer if you turn out to be a minimalist who just bought out four aisles of cycle-shop goods. Instead of buying everything in the store you *think* you'll need during your cycling adventures, you should start out with a few things you *know* you'll need and then return later, as your needs become more clear.

Part of the point of training is for you to figure out exactly what you need and like on your rides. It didn't take long for me to figure out that I needed and liked all downhill routes. When you first start riding, you aren't going to be heading out for fifty-mile rides right away, so you can use those first short rides to home in on what's best for you. Start making mental notes of the different things you're having trouble with (breathing), and then see if there is a product out there that might help you out (iron lung). Talk to your fellow cyclists out on the routes and get their opinions, too. The best accessory recommendations for newbies will come from people who survived their newbie phase and have tips on how you can, too.

Also, remember that cycling is not a cheap sport. This is a difficult reality to avoid. Most of the things you are going to need are going to be found only at cycle shops, and cycle shops aren't exactly known for their affordability. I once bought a cycling shirt *on clearance* for $60. Then I cried (while my credit card company rejoiced). The good news is that most of the expenses for the sport are pretty front-heavy. After your initial gathering of all the things you need, ongoing costs are actually fairly minimal. That's a nice thing to keep in mind when you find yourself having to sell a kidney in order to afford the start-up costs of cycling. It might

•

also be good motivation to actually stick with the sport. It would be a shame to lose a major organ for a hobby you gave up after three weeks.

Below, I've broken up the bike accessories into different categories, from most important to "that sounds cool."

Have to Haves

The *have to have* items are things you should buy when you get your bike. You are going to need them from ride one. I guess you could technically be like me and just head out on your first ride with a bike and great cycling ambitions and hope for the best, but I think we all know that being like me isn't going to get you very far. Literally. Because I found myself stranded on my first ride with a flat tire and no way to fix it. (It was at that point when my cycling ambitions got downgraded from "great" to merely "moving.")

This is a bare-bones list of the minimum essentials you should have when heading out for the first ride. It was made on the assumption that the primary goal of your first ride is to actually finish it. The list below will help you make that dream a reality, keeping both your body and your bike full of what they need: water and air, respectively.

WATER BOTTLES/CAGES

As we all know, hydration is of the utmost importance when you are moving your body and sweating out gallons of water from your head and armpits. Your bike is prepared to aid you in your hydration efforts and has allowed a couple of spaces where water-bottle cages can be attached. You'll need to buy both the cages and the water bottles to put in them. Make sure you do this so that you're heading off on your rides with plenty of water at your fingertips. I'm sure you can attach the cages yourself, but I had the Bike Maintenance Dude do it for me in the store, since my mechanical skills are similar to my athletic skills and I didn't want to see what happened when I tried to combine the two on my first foray into cycling.

On your first couple of rides, which will be relatively short, you can use one of your water bottles for water and the other as a storage container. Throw your keys, some cash, and some flat tire–fixing materials in there and be on your merry way. This isn't the most ideal of storage locations, since everything in the bottle will be bouncing around and making annoying noises for the duration of your trip. But for the sake of bare-bonesing it, your bottle can make a handy little storage container if needed.

SPARE TUBES

This should probably be number one on the list, because you won't need much hydration if you have a flat tire. Even if you don't know how to change a tire, you need spare tubes so that the nice people who stop to help you change your tire actually have something to change the flat into. Get the tubes when you get the bike, so that you are sure to get the right kinds of tubes for your tires. I'd recommend getting four of them; that way, you won't have to return during your training for more. Hopefully. (If you do run out of tubes, you may also be cursed with horrible tire karma, and you might want to consider taking up a less roll-y sport.)

LEVERS

These are the handy little tools that you use to change your flat tires. They are about three inches long and flat on one end. This allows you to maneuver them between your tire and the rim, prying the tire away so you can get to and replace the flat tube inside.

PUMP OR CO$_2$

Once you replace that flat tube inside your tire, you are going to need to fill it somehow (tubes don't transport so well if they are already full of air before you leave the house). There are a few options for getting air into your tires, so you need to decide which one you want to go with, at least initially. The most basic option is a pump, either one that attaches to the frame of your bike or one that is smaller and can fit in a pocket or other storage device on your bike. If you get a pump that is supposed to be mounted on your bike, make sure it actually fits your bike and that it's mounted correctly (another possible job for Bike Maintenance Dude). Pumps that don't fit correctly have a tendency to take leave of a bike ride at the most inconvenient times, usually resulting in a swerving cyclist behind you or, at the very least, a grumbling cyclist (that would be you) having to turn around and gather up the escaped pump.

Pumps are useful and get the job done, but can also be somewhat difficult to use if you are anything like me and are stricken with the upper-body strength of a weak chicken. Years of your life can pass by while you are trying to inflate a tire one pathetic pump at a time. A quicker option for those of the weak-chicken or merely impatient variety are CO$_2$ cartridges. They are tiny little

cartridges full of compressed air, and they will fill your tires ridiculously quickly. Unlike a pump that can be used again and again,
CO_2 cartridges are a one-time-use apparatus. This can present a
problem if you have more than one flat tire.

Your best bet for filling your tubes is to consider one of the
products that combines the CO_2 with a pump, giving you the
quickness of the CO_2 and the reliability of a pump.

Probably Should Haves

The following are things you probably should get at some point
in your training, but won't necessarily need to buy the very first
time you enter the cycle shop. Take your bike on some rides first,
figure out which of the items below you need, and then head to
the store to pick them up.

SADDLEBAG

A saddlebag is not so much a bag as a little pouch sort of thing
that fits under the back of your bike seat. Considering how small
it looks, it actually fits quite a bit of stuff in it and is a nifty storage compartment. I can fit my cell phone, some cash, my flat-tire
stuff, and some snacks in my saddlebag. This is the best and most
compact way to store your necessities as you ride along.

SADDLE

The seat of your bike is called the saddle, like you put on a horse.
Except it's a lot smaller, harder, and less comfortable, and results in
no galloping (unless you count the weird dance you may do after
you pry yourself off an uncomfortable saddle following a long

ride). Your bike will come with a saddle, so there is no need to purchase a new one right away, but you may need to eventually if your first saddle isn't working for you.

Saddles on road bikes are ridiculously hard and not at all like the fat, soft ones on cruiser bikes. I've been told this is intentional because they're supposed to provide more comfort and support to the rider. I've even heard tales of how hard saddles feel better than soft ones. I pass this information on to you because it was given to me by smart bike people, but I will also point out that providing comfort didn't seem to be a top priority for the saddles my buttocks came into contact with.

Saddles are definitely something that shouldn't be changed too early in your training. When you first get into cycling, it is inevitable that your ass is going to hurt. That isn't so much because you have a bad saddle as because your butt isn't comfortable on anything besides a recliner. If, after a couple weeks of riding, you are still in a lot of pain, you should visit the Bike Dudes and get recommendations for another saddle. I've heard of cyclists going through fifteen saddles before they found one that was comfortable. I personally tried two before I realized that I'm comfortable only when lying down watching cable, and the odds weren't good that I was going to find a saddle that replicated that scenario.

LOCK

Not everyone is going to need a lock during their cycling adventures. It depends on where you are doing your riding and where you commonly leave your bike unattended. I think I used a bike lock twice in the duration of my training, which isn't a great return on investment for the $50 lock I bought. If you are doing most of your rides on bike trails and don't leave your bike unattended during your training, then a lock might not even be necessary. But at the very least you'll probably want to get a cable lock that wraps easily around the frame of your bike and will go pretty much unnoticed until you need it. It might be handy to have for that one time you impulsively decide to pull over and visit an all-you-can-eat Chinese buffet at mile 25 of a long ride (although when I did this, the nice waiters let me bring my bike inside with me, which was very helpful).

The super-duper U locks are, coincidently, U-shaped and weigh as much as a small automobile. They are great for protecting your bike in city environments, where you may leave it unattended for long periods of time. But if you aren't planning on needing this kind of lock, it can add a lot of unnecessary weight to your load and might be better left at home or, better yet, in the cycle shop.

LIGHTS

Lights are important to help you see, but more important to help you be seen. Lights are one of those things you probably won't really think about until you are in a situation where you should probably have some. This situation will usually present itself around the time the sun sets and you are officially an undetectable moving object who is trying to share the road with motorists.

If you are doing all of your riding during the day and have no intention of ever riding at night, lights aren't going to be that important for you. However, there are some lights that go on the back of your bike and flash continuously. Those aren't a bad idea for both day- and nighttime, just because their flashing is kinda annoying and therefore bound to get the attention of drivers. Anything that helps drivers become aware of your presence is going to help you stay unflattened by a car. If you are a commuter, or are thinking of going on any evening rides, lights are mandatory. There is a group in my town that does some fun rides in the evening, and they require everyone to have lights on their bikes before they're allowed to ride. And an exemplary group of cyclists they are.

There are a lot of different lights in various locations on your bike and power source. Some cool ones are actually powered by your bike itself, which is a nice feature because you don't have to worry about batteries running out and leaving you wandering the streets in the dark.

PATCH KIT

This is a small kit that includes patching materials for a punctured tube. Instead of replacing a flat tube with a new tube, you also have the option of simply patching the hole in the flat tube. These kits have a super glue-type material, as well as small patches, for your tube. I've found the patches to be hit or miss: Some people ride around on tubes with multiple patches for quite some time, and other people's patched tires go flat immediately after the rider starts pedaling again. If you don't mind spending the extra time, it's worth a shot to try to patch up a tire, only because if it works, you'll save yourself from having to use up a spare tube. But if you just want to change your flat and get on with your life, I'd say throw a new tube in there and be on your happy way.

FLOOR PUMP

Tires will actually go flat from just sitting in your garage, waiting for you to ride on them. It's as if they lose their cycling excitement at the same time you do. You can fill up your tired tires with your hand pump, but it's not an easy task, and by the time you are done you will most likely need a nap and will have lost all interest in the actual riding.

Floor pumps are a quick, easy way to fill up your tires before your rides; they also have a handy gauge mounted on them so you can be sure that your tire pressure is correct. These pumps don't come cheap, so if you don't want to splurge on one, you'll probably want to get used to stopping by your local cycle shop before each big ride. They'll usually fill you up for free, but that added stop before you get on your bike can be a bit of a pain.

CLIPLESS PEDALS

It's possible that your bike won't even come with pedals, as some of the fancy-shmancy bikes don't. If your bike doesn't, then go ahead and add "pedals" to the "have to have" list above, as I don't think any of the rest of the stuff on this list matters if you aren't able to pedal the bike. Many cyclists consider clipless pedals a must-have because there are lots of bike enthusiasts who couldn't · imagine riding long distances without them. Clipless pedals are small, roundish pedals that replace normal bike pedals. The genius of these pedals is that they click into the bottom of special riding shoes, attaching the shoe (and you) to the pedal.

This means that unlike regular pedals, which give you the benefit of your downward leg motion only, clipless pedals also power your bike forward with the motion of pulling your leg back up. In addition to the added fun of being clipped into your pedal, clipless pedals also force your foot to stay in exactly the right spot and holds it there for maximum power and results. You will basically be a riding machine after you get these pedals, and not a moment before.

Clipless pedals do take a little getting used to, as they essentially attach your foot to the bike and can leave you feeling at a loss for control. There's a learning curve with these as you get used to clipping and unclipping your shoes, and you will most likely fall at least once during that curve. (You might want to try the pedals out for the first time near soft shoulders.) But in the end, clipless pedals are a great benefit to your long-distance rides and are worth the effort to get used to.

One downside to these pedals is that they aren't super easy to get in and out of. If you are riding in heavy traffic areas and require quick stops and dismounts from your bike, clipless pedals will not be a good fit for you. Also, some of the shoes required for riding with clipless pedals are great on the bike but loud and clumsy on land. When buying shoes, look for the kind that are made to be walked around in. They are still a little awkward, but they won't make you feel like a total dork when you are seen (and heard) while walking around on breaks or following your ride.

Your Choice

There are quite a few extras that can be added on to your bike if you are in the mood to spend money and want to see how much stuff you can fit on your two-wheeled friend. Some of these things are more fun than functional (I still think streamers could make a comeback), but they are all eagerly awaiting your impulse buy. Below are a few extras you might want to spring for, if you are so inclined.

TOUGHER TIRES

Nice road bikes usually come with good tires, but if you are experiencing a lot of flats, or are just paranoid about experiencing a lot of flats, then you might want to consider getting slightly tougher, heavier tires. Unless you are a supercyclist, you will not notice much difference between the lighter and heavier tires. Supercyclists will note that the heavier-duty tires slow down your performance time, but I might note that sitting on the side of the road with a flat is not a great way to set any cycling records, either.

REARVIEW MIRROR

Some people enjoy rearview mirrors and can't imagine riding without them. Others have just gotten good at looking over their shoulder without veering their bike into a tree and/or oncoming automobile. You know best what category you fall into.

Rearview mirrors come in different designs; some clip onto your handlebars, and others clip onto your helmet. Both take a little getting used to and can actually be a distraction to some riders (perhaps it's better not to know exactly how close cars come to hitting you).

I never realized how much I use my rearview mirrors in my car until I got on my bike and was constantly looking around for a mirror to tell me what was going on behind me. Then, when I bought a couple mirrors for my bike, I found it very difficult to use them effectively. I could never quite get them adjusted perfectly, and I always ended up having to move my head around to try to get the correct angle for seeing behind me. All this moving and adjusting for the sake of things going on behind me took quite a bit of time away from my awareness of the things going on in front of me, which was not an acceptable sacrifice, in my opinion. I gave up on the mirrors and instead just started doing a lot of praying that I wouldn't get hit. So far, the prayers seem to be working, because I haven't been run over yet. Thanks, Big Guy.

COMPUTER

A wide variety of cycling computers are available, no matter what kind of cyclist you are. The computers range in functionality from telling you how many miles you've ridden to using GPS software to map out your routes. Computers are definitely a helpful addition to your training efforts, because they will spit out all sorts of information and facts that will help you gauge exactly how your rides are going. Facts range from your speed to your distance to your heart rate, and quite possibly, the long-term prospects of your 401(k) investments. In other words, they are knowledgeable.

If you are planning on doing any sort of bicycle touring, computers make it easier to navigate the mileage on your route sheets, which can be extremely comforting when you are wandering the barren countryside all by yourself. There are also cool websites that work with the cycling GPS and allow you to upload and download bike routes and trips. The computer will keep track of where you went and how you got there, and then you can upload your route to different websites so that others can view where you've been, and even download and take the trip themselves.

It's kinda like MapQuest, except you look up ways to be active, instead of getting directions to the closest Mexican restaurant.

Some people can't get enough of computers and numbers and specifics. These people are tech geeks and will absolutely flip over the exciting things a cycling computer can do. Overall, computers are a great way to monitor your progress and get hard data on your cycling abilities. The hard data on my cycling abilities is what always deterred me from getting a computer. The fact that I spent most of my training being passed by every cyclist on the road was pretty much all the hard data I needed to gather about my abilities and overall training progress.

The above-mentioned items are the basics for your bike and overall cycling fun and excitement. There is no need to buy every one of them, or to put yourself into a financial crisis for the sake of cycling. While it's difficult to find many of these items for cheap at the stores, you might consider looking on Craigslist or in other classified ads to see if there are people in your area who might be giving up on their cycling dreams and have therefore decided to sell all the crap they bought and never really used. Barely used crap will usually go for a decent price, and your new athletic aspirations can benefit from the dissolution of another person's. It's the circle of life, really.

While I'm a big fan of spreading out your accessory purchases, I will also warn you that you are going to need to be a strong soul in order for this strategy to actually save you money. First of all, you are going to have to be strong enough to not buy every other product for sale on the day you purchase your bike. Then you are going to have to be even stronger when you return to the store to gather up some things you've decided you need. The key is to go into the shop and get what you need, then exit the shop. No dilly-dallying. Because dilly-dallying leads to irrational beliefs that you *need* a lot more things than you actually do. And then you wake up from a purchasing stupor back in your car with five bags and a credit card receipt totaling $650. This could be exponentially worse if you are taking my advice and visiting the cycle shop regularly. Eventually you are going to have to make a tent out of cycling jerseys when you are unable to afford your mortgage payment because of your lack of purchasing willpower. And even that isn't going to work out well, because cycling jerseys are crappy at keeping out the elements.

If you know that you are the kind of person who is easily lured into impulse buying, then you very well might be better off stocking up on all the accessories you may need in one or two visits to the bike shop. You will probably end up with things you don't actually use, but in the long run it may save you from buying even more things you don't need.

Pimp Yourself

O nce you have adequately weighed down your bike with all things accessory and shiny, it is time to turn your attention toward your body and the precise combination of biking apparel that is needed to turn you into a superstar. (I warn you that one of the major pieces of apparel involves spandex, so you will probably look like a superstar of the 1980s hair-band variety.)

Buying accessories for your body can get a little out of hand and is therefore often the area in which you end up spending way too much money. While accessories for the bike itself can be expensive, you typically don't need to buy more than one of each item. However, with body accessories it is very easy to convince yourself that you not only need a certain item, but also need it in several colors. This is where things start to get out of hand.

On your first trip to the cycle shop, you must be strong and not buy every single cute thing you see. Yes, I know the color variations make the accessories look different, make them completely different products, but for the sake of your financial stability, please try to control yourself.

Following is a list of some things that might lead you into quite a bit of credit card debt while helping you look adorable at the same time.

Have to Haves

HELMET

Helmets are a must-have, because you must have your brain inside your head in order to live a full life. Helmets are a little bit of a pain to get used to, since on the whole you are not used to having things on your head or cinched around your neck. But eventually it will become second nature to throw one on before heading out for a ride. (It will never become any nature, however, to appreciate the horrible hair you are left with after you finish your ride and take the helmet off.)

Helmets range wildly in price, for no real reason other than that people are willing to pay a stupid amount of money for cycling accessories. Do not be one of these people. Every helmet has to pass the same safety tests and adhere to Keep Cyclists' Brains on the Inside of Their Heads guidelines (or something equally official sounding), so spending more money on a helmet isn't going to make your head any safer when it meets concrete. More-expensive helmets can offer a slightly more comfortable fit, as well as some snazzier design elements. Snazzy costs more to produce, apparently.

Make sure you buy a helmet specific to the type of riding you will be doing. Road biking and mountain biking helmets have vents that are laid out slightly differently because the ventilation you require while participating in these two types of cycling varies. This is not a huge deal, but I'm a big fan of anything involving the word "ventilation" when I'm participating in athletic activities, and I figure I can use all the help I can get in that area.

SHORTS

When you start cycling, butt soreness is going to be the biggest complaint you have. Without bike shorts, you'd find that your complaint would probably turn into loud screaming and possibly some violence toward your bike seat.

Bike shorts provide padding to protect your poor bum and private parts while you're out riding. They also provide a glimpse into how it will feel to wear adult diapers, which is a treat. By "protect," I mean they will soften the hurt a little, because cycling shorts in no way eliminate all of the pain you will feel following your entry into the world of sitting on a hard object for hours at a time.

Cycling shorts have gender-specific padding that protects male and female bodies differently. They are also made of wicking material that will keep you dry while you're riding, and they can be washed and dried quickly.

Cycling shorts can be purchased in a few different styles. There is the ever-popular spandex style, which leaves you and your newly padded butt out for the world to see. The spandex style comes in short, long, and lovely full-body models. The short version is the most common, while the long shorts are usually worn in colder climates to keep cyclists' legs warm. The full-body shorts eliminate the tight elastic waistband and instead stay on your body via a bib, which is actually more like a suspender contraption. The end result leaves you wearing something that looks like the leotards weight lifters don while holding six hundred pounds over their heads. If you go for the always popular "lift your bike over your head to show your cycling power" photo opportunity while wearing full-body shorts, you will actually look a lot like those weight lifters. Minus the protruding veins (hopefully).

If you're not feeling the spandexed-buttocks look, there are some mountain biking shorts available for the sole purpose, it seems, of covering up the spandex. They usually have the tight bike shorts woven into baggier shorts, a feature that allows you to ride without being self-conscious. These are not bad for shorter rides, but when you get up into higher mileage, these pants might start to annoy you. There are actual reasons why bike shorts are so tight, and one of those reasons is that baggier shorts will bunch up while you are riding and cause you even more problems.

It's probably a good idea to buy two or three pairs of bike shorts on your first trip to the cycle shop. You can use those three over and over again throughout your training. However, please note that they are not meant to be worn with underwear, so make sure you wash them after each use, because they can get pretty funky after protecting your butt for hours at a time.

Probably Should Haves

JERSEYS

Cycling jerseys are shirts made specifically for cyclists. They are made of synthetic fibers and usually have bright colors or wild patterns on them, which make you more noticeable to motorists and various wildlife. Cycling jerseys usually feature a handy little zipper on the front that you can open and close based on the temperature. The jerseys are also a little longer in the back, so that when you are bent over in your race to the finish line you aren't flashing your back to everyone behind you (not that there was ever anyone left *behind* me when I was racing to the finish line). In addition to being long, the back usually has a little kangaroo-type pouch where you can fit Goo or your cell phone or cash for beer.

Cycling jerseys are definitely a cool thing to have and are quite functional, what with their secret storage compartments and whatnot. But I put them in the *probably should have* category because you can do just fine without a shirt made specifically for cycling. The only thing to remember is that you shouldn't wear cotton shirts. Make sure you wear shirts made from synthetic fibers that will help keep your skin dry of sweat. I cycled quite a bit in shirts I had left over from my marathon-training heyday. They worked just fine, even though I did drop a few things on the ground when I reached back to put them in my kangaroo pouch that didn't exist.

If you are going to buy cycling jerseys, I'd highly recommend waiting for sales or clearances. Unlike running shirts, I've never found any super-cheap cycling jerseys, so clearances are going to be your only hope of not spending three figures on a friggin' shirt. The good news is that the friggin' shirts are well made and won't need to be replaced during your training, or even for years afterward (sitting in a closet doesn't cause much wear and tear on a jersey, as it turns out). Jerseys are the items most likely to cause mass purchasing, too, because of their different pretty colors and fun designs. But you must be stronger than the style and limit yourself to only a couple of jerseys, at least initially. They are fine to wear often and sometimes even without washing in between rides (if you ride like me and do a lot more swearing than sweating).

SHOES

Unless you are using clipless pedals, you don't really need special riding shoes right off the bat, although there are many types available and each will probably promise to help you immensely. As you get further along in your mileage, the benefits of special shoes will become more apparent. Cycling shoes have stiff soles that maximize your pedaling power and keep your feet from getting too sore from all the spinning.

There's a huge variety of cycling shoes at cycle shops: shoes made specifically for road riding and ones made for mountain biking as well. I've seen the mountain biking shoes used by road cyclists, but have never seen the road shoes used by mountain bikers. Some road cyclists prefer mountain biking shoes because they are easier to ride in following the actual ride. Also, if you are planning on doing any bike touring or will need to walk around in your shoes for any period of time after your ride, you might want to consider the shoes that are now available with soles that are slightly less stiff and look a little like tennis shoes. They are much easier to walk around in and won't require you to bring an extra pair of running shoes to walk in when you're not on the bike.

GLOVES

Theoretically, you can ride a bike without cycling gloves, and I actually did a good portion of my training without them (I'm hardcore like that). But the world opened up in a lovely way the first time I threw some on my poor, shaken hands.

The gloves are fingerless and have pads along your palms that help absorb the abundant vibrations that will be coming from your handlebars. You don't even realize how much vibration is coming from those handlebars until you get off the bike and your hands continue to vibrate for another thirty minutes. These vibrations and shakes can affect your arms and neck, and gloves help alleviate that a little.

For those of you who plan on falling off your bike (and you should all plan on falling off your bike, so that when you do you can chalk it up to being part of your training plan), the cycling gloves' padding will help soften the blow a little bit.

BUTT BUTTER

As I mentioned earlier, your butt is going to be your biggest issue during your cycling adventures. Several products are available to help in your efforts to avoid complete butt breakdown, and Butt Butter is one of them. I am recommending this particular product because I enjoy the name, but there are many others that accomplish the same task. Basically, they are like Vaseline and provide a slippery buffer between you and your shorts, alleviating rashes and soreness caused by chafing. You will see many cyclists with their hands down their pants before races, applying one of these products to their nether regions. Join them in the ritual and become one of the cool kids.

Your Choice

GLASSES

There are cycling-specific glasses that have shatterproof lenses and grips in the right places to keep them from falling off your head. You should definitely wear glasses of some sort, because you will be traveling at high speeds, and wind and random bugs are not

good times when they hit your eyeballs. If you already have favorite glasses, you will probably be fine leaving cycling glasses off
your list. They look cool and aerodynamic, but your $5 minimart
glasses will probably suit you just fine. I have prescription glasses
and simply wore those throughout my training and rides. I'm sure
I would have been happier with cycling sunglasses, but I'm also
sure I would have crashed into at least twelve trees because I'm
uselessly blind without my prescription lenses.

CAMELBAKS

CamelBaks are the most popular brand of backpack with a plastic
pouch for carrying water. A CamelBak is quite handy because it
also has a little tube that carries the water over your shoulder and
into your mouth (I'm eagerly awaiting the updated CamelBak
that will pump some air into my lungs). If you are like me and
risk death every time you reach down to grab your water bottle
off your bike, the CamelBak can provide a convenient way for
you to hydrate while maintaining your balance and well-being.
The backpack has space for storing other, nonhydrating items as
well, providing you with another way to carry snacks and your
cell phone.

CamelBaks are quite convenient, but they do add a little discomfort to your ride, at least until you completely get used to
wearing one. The times I wore one, I wasn't a big fan of the extra
weight on my back and also found myself getting hotter because
the backpack was trapping in the heat my back usually lets off.
But when I wore the CamelBak through the busy streets of New
York City, I was very happy to have a quick hydration option that
didn't require me to stop or let go of my brakes at all. Without

a CamelBak, I very well might have died in New York and been found days later lying on the side of a street, completely dehydrated but still grasping my brakes violently.

I will also warn you that CamelBaks are not popular among supercyclists, and some may ride in silent judgment of you for having one. For me, though, it was just one more thing on the list of things real cyclists could criticize me for.

Special Cold-Weather Attire

I live in California and am not a fan of or experienced with exercising in cold temperatures. (Well, I do exercise in what feels cold to me, but that temperature would probably be laughed, possibly even snorted, at by those who live in climates a little less sunny than dear old California's). But for those of you who made the unfortunate decision to live somewhere with actual winters, there are quite a few options to help you cycle happily during those cold months. Option one: Move to California.

The biggest problem with cycling in the cold is that not only is it cold outside, but you are also engaging in a sport that is moving very fast through that cold, which makes you even colder. Like those weather forecasts that say the temperature is 70 degrees but it "feels like" 72 degrees, riding in the cold can "feel like" you are going to die of hypothermia in forty-five seconds' time.

The best tip for riding in the cold is to layer your clothes. This will provide you with some shelter from the elements, but will also allow you to strip down gradually if you become warmer. You don't want your only options to be a parka or nudity when you're riding to work on a cold day. (FYI: Always go with the parka in that particular situation.) In addition to layering, there are some products made specifically for you crazy winter riders.

JACKETS

There are a lot of different styles of jackets, not all made specifically for really cold temperatures. Sometimes it's nice to have a thin windbreaker to wear over your jersey to lessen the amount of wind that's hitting your skin. If you live in really cold climates, there are winter-specific jackets that will keep all of the elements out and leave you toasty on the inside. They are also designed with fun features that protect your butt and allow you to open little ventilation slits if you need to cool down a bit.

ARM/LEG WARMERS

Arm and leg warmers are a nice alternative to wearing a jacket in cold weather. The arm warmers are basically sleeves that provide warmth and protection, and they are quite useful because they are easy to get on and off while you're riding, and are very compact and transportable. The leg warmers are equally helpful, though not quite as easy to get in and out of, since they require you to lift your leg off the pedal to put them on. So unless you pull them off by lifting your leg above your head while cycling, you're probably going to have to get off your bike.

Both of these are good options for rides that may start off cold and end up warm. Most people use only the arm warmers, since their legs can handle a little cold. I've also heard of people taking the arm warmers on long flights when temperatures can get a little chilly. Again, the leg warmers might not go over quite as well in this situation, as it might appear as though you are removing your pants on the plane. This could lead to some sort of tackling by a highly trained counter-terrorism official aboard the plane.

GLOVES WITH FINGERS

Standard cycling gloves come fingerless, but there are some available that will cover your entire hand and keep your little fingers safe from the rain and wind.

BEANIE/HEADBAND

A bike helmet is designed to let air stream through it, so it is not the best at stopping the cold from hitting your head. You can wear a beanie under your helmet that covers part or all of your head. This will help trap some of the heat that your head is giving off and use it to warm the rest of your body. If the beanie is a little too claustrophobic for you, consider wearing a headband around your ears to protect them from the whizzing wind.

FOOT WARMERS/BOOTIES

Your cycling shoes, like all your other athletic accessories, are designed to let your body breathe. But when it's cold outside your body wants to snuggle up next to a fire, not breathe in the freezing temperatures. When you're riding in cold or rainy weather, there are a few products that slip over your shoe and keep them toasty and dry. These are a must-have in cold climates because cold, wet feet are proven to be the beginning of many an irritable and disgruntled thought.

Buying Tip

While I recommend spacing out your accessories purchases so that you can make educated decisions about what you actually need, I will also tell you that the most important part of your training is getting used to the accessories you do end up buying. You should have pretty much all of your major accessories about a month into training. That way, you can spend the rest of your training getting used to these products and allowing them to get used to you. They have to mold to your body and become worn in in just the right places so that you will be comfortable with them when your mileage gets ridiculously high, or at least as comfortable as one can be when mileage becomes ridiculous. Good luck!

Taking Care of the Bike

S ome people get into cycling and get plain *giddy* about bike maintenance. A friend of mine spends hours in his garage, just staring at and fidgeting with his bike. Another guy I know actually *makes* bike tires. These people obviously don't know how much reality television they are missing, but to each his own, I guess. If you feel so inclined, there are books upon books that offer you information galore about the wondrous workings of your two-wheeled piece of metal and how you can become one with every bolt and spoke. You can also take a bike-maintenance class that will offer you hands-on information and support. But then again, there's no need to get crazy.

Perhaps you are like me and maintain a healthy "isn't there some sort of professional who can do this for me?" attitude toward all things even sorta mechanical. But if changing the batteries in your television remote is about as technically advanced as you get, you are going to need to pick up a few tips of the maintenance variety to make sure your bike runs smoothly.

All major issues you have with your bike (say, the seat falling off) should be directed toward Bike Maintenance Dudes, but there are several tiny things that you can do regularly that will help your bike live long and prosper. (I imagine keeping the seat from falling off is going to go a long way in helping *you* prosper as well.)

Lube

There are several different kinds of bike lubes available for different riding types and conditions. It's best to go into your local bike shop and ask for advice about what lube is best for you, based on where and when you'll be riding your bike. But whatever lube you decide to go with, it's important to lube up your chain and other moving parts of your bike every few weeks or so, or after the bike has gotten wet (from rain, or perhaps an unfortunate turn into the neighborhood pond), because water will remove the lube you've applied.

In order to lube your chain, you should flip your bike over, resting it on its handlebars and seat with the wheels in the air. Then apply the lube to the chain as you slowly pedal backward using your hands. Put a lot of lube on the chain, wait for it to settle in a bit, and then use a rag to wipe away the excess. The lube is supposed to seep into the chain, not exist on the outside of it, so you want to get as much of the excess off as possible.

It's also a good idea to lightly lube any other moving parts of your bike, such as levers and derailleurs.

Tires

A friend of mine who used to be a bike mechanic said that tire issues outnumbered any other maintenance requests he received by nearly 4 to 1. And I've done an informal study to deduct that *having* tire issues outweighs good times by nearly 75,863 to 1. So it's really in your best interest to pay close attention to your tires and do everything you can to make them happy.

Before you head out on a ride, check your tire pressure and make sure your tires are filled to the correct level. Also, examine the tire, checking for any holes, tears, or even dry and cracked sidewalls. Tires wear down and need to be replaced, so keep an eye on yours so that an explosion at mile 27 isn't the point at which you realize that a replacement might be overdue.

Another quick thing to do before you take off on a ride is to stand in front of your tire and spin it, making sure it's spinning straight and isn't touching the brake pads, which could lead to friction galore and the above-mentioned explosion.

Brakes

Before you head out, do a quick test of your brakes to make sure they are actually squeezing your tire when you squeeze the brake levers on your handlebars. Also, check to make sure your brake pads are actually still pads and haven't worn down to metal. You will benefit from examining these small but important brake features before you are careening down a ridiculously steep hill.

Clean the Bike

Even if you are just riding around town, your bike can get dirt and residue built up in its different parts. Left unattended, this buildup can eventually become a problem and cause your bike's various moving parts to not move so well. Depending on your riding circumstances and location, you may or may not need to clean your bike often. Simply take a look at the bike every week or so and clean it if it looks like it's getting a little too dirty.

You can clean your bike just like you would a car, with a hose, soap, and water, or you can simply use a wet rag to wipe it down. If you do spray the bike down, do so gently and remember that you'll need to relube the chains afterward, because you will have sprayed all the lube away.

Once a Year

Just like any piece of machinery, a bike needs to be looked at by a professional every once in a while, if for no other reason than peace of mind. At least once a year, take your bike in for a tune-up. The Bike Maintenance Dudes will give your bike a complete working over, taking it apart and putting it back together again, much like it's Humpty Dumpty—if Humpty Dumpty had been very well lubed (which would have made his balancing on that wall even more precarious). Unlike Mr. Dumpty, your bike will be much better for the reassembly and will reward you with top-notch performance and shinyness.

More than anything, be aware of your bike and take time to give it a good once-over before every ride. Don't just hop on and assume that it will work perfectly without any attention from you at all. Think of it as a high-maintenance friend—a little attention now and then will help you avoid a huge explosion down the road. Also, would it kill you to give it a hug every once in a while?

Gimme a Bike

I have officially begun my foray into cycling with the purchase of a shiny new bike. I'd been meaning to get a bike for a while now, but I just never quite got around to it. Honestly, I was a bit intimidated by the whole process, afraid that I was going to end up making the wrong choice and then be left with a horrible bike whose enthusiasm for movement matched mine (meaning it would have none). I needed a superbike that, with the strength of its wheels and the slickness of its design, would lead me to cycling victory (and by "victory," I mean it would just lead me to cycling, period).

One day, while visiting my thirteen-year-old cousin, Katy, in Davis, California, I became obsessed with making my bike purchase. Davis is a college town and probably has as many bikes as it does cars, so I figured I'd be able to find a good bike there. The town probably has more bike shops per capita than any place on the planet, so that had to mean that they were good shops, right? Right.

Katy was bored, so she decided to walk to the bike shop with me, hoping to be a part of the beginning of my biking odyssey (and also to make fun of me for my complete lack of knowledge regarding bikes).

We got to the store and were immediately greeted by a friendly Bike Girl who walked up to us to see if she could be of assistance. "I need a bike," I said, with great specificity.

"What kind of bike?" she asked patiently.

"I need to ride really far on it."

"Really far where? On the road?"

>>>

"Yes, I don't think you are supposed to ride on the sidewalk."

"No, as opposed to off-road, mountain bikes."

"Oh, yes. No, I'm riding on the road, unless I'm buzzed by a car and fall off the road." I smiled at my own joke.

"Uh-huh." She did not smile at my joke. She led us over to the bikes. "What is your price range?"

I shrugged. "How much do bikes cost?"

She pointed to different bikes, naming different prices. Some of these prices were much more than my mortgage, which scared me a bit. That seemed like a lot of money to spend on something I could very well lose interest in. In fact, seeing how much bikes cost was already causing me to lose interest.

Then I saw a pretty bike hanging from a rack down the aisle a bit and pointed to it. "How about that one? The black one with the flowers on it? That one is cool."

She pulled the bike down and I took a look at the price. It was less than my mortgage *and* it had pretty flowers painted on it. What more could I ask for?

"I like this one," I proclaimed.

"Do you want to take it for a test ride or something first, before you buy it?"

"Oh, I can do that?"

"Uh, yeah."

Katy was very excited about my hopping on the bike and riding around the parking lot. A tiny giggle came from her mouth, until I shot her a glare—at which point a very large giggle came out. Kids.

The nice Bike Girl put me against some sort of tall computer contraption, which measured different things on my body and then spit out a piece of paper full of my personal information. Bike Girl then took that information and did several things to my shiny bike to make it fit me, or something. Then I was off on my test-drive, ready to fall even more in love with this fine piece of metal.

I rode around for a little while, not really knowing what I was supposed to be checking out, exactly. I knew the seat was hard and uncomfortable, but I'd heard that was normal. And Lord knows I was used to athletic activities being uncomfortable, so that hardly deterred me. I pedaled fast, then slow, then fast again. I used the brakes. They worked. This all seemed like good news to me, so I rode back to where my cousin and Bike Girl were waiting. "Seems good to me."

"It doesn't feel like it needs any adjustments?" Bike Girl asked.

I looked at the bike intently, as if examining it thoroughly, when in fact I was just looking at the pretty flowers painted on it, "Um, yeah, I don't think so. Seems good to go."

Bike Girl smiled and rolled the bike back into the shop. I followed her up to the cash register and got my credit card out, ready to make my purchase. She looked at me and frowned slightly. "Did you want to get a helmet?"

A helmet! Of course!

"And do you have any bike shorts or shirts?" she asked.

I put my credit card back in my purse. "Yes, I should probably get some things besides just the bike."

Katy and I wandered around the store, picking up various bike whatnots, afraid to return to the checkout counter

>>>

without all the things a good cyclist is supposed to have. I tried on some cycling shorts and laughed at the sight of my ass covered in spandex once again. After my marathon training, my butt and I had made an agreement to never be near spandex again. It had been traumatizing for the both of us. And yet here I was, once again turning around in the dressing room, looking at my backside in the mirror, trying to find a magical pair of cycling shorts that somehow looked good. This was a nearly impossible task, seeing as how cycling shorts include all the fun and excitement of running shorts but have the added feature of butt padding. When I see my ass in spandex, the first thing I think is, *Man, if only I could somehow get some padding involved here, this look could really start working.*

After I looked at the price tag on the padded-butt shorts, I examined the padding again, convinced that perhaps there was a computerized device hidden inside—or, at the very least, a valuable mineral of some sort. Because if not, I was about to spend nearly a hundred dollars for the privilege of exposing a padded version of my ass to the general public. This seemed like all sorts of unjust.

After I regained my composure following the realization that being a cycling superstar was going to max out my credit cards, I finished up my accessory accumulation and returned to the checkout counter. Katy and I plopped down the various items we'd loaded into our arms and looked at Bike Girl for approval. She glanced over the pile, then looked to me. "All set?" Bike Girl is not easily impressed, it turns out.

I nodded. "I've got everything I need."

>>>

>>>

Katy smirked. "Now all you need to do is actually *ride* the bike."

I did not smirk back, "I've got earmuffs, rearview mirrors, and butt pads—I'm halfway home."

Katy, again with the smirk, just nodded. "Uh-huh, right."

Kids.

CHAPTER *two*

The Training

The Century Schedule

The truth is that training for a one-hundred-mile ride, commonly known as a century ride, can be summed up in two steps.

Step one: Ride a lot.

Step two: Ride some more.

But sometimes people need a little more detailed training program to adhere to when tackling a major athletic event. In the interest of those people, I enlisted the help of a professional (I know, it's hard to believe after reading my two-step century training program that I'm not a professional myself) to help guide you with details aplenty.

Mike Beretta, PT, ATC, USACC (and other acronyms), is the owner of both Revolutions Cycling Center and Beretta Physical Therapy, near Sacramento, California. (If Mike also owned a bar, he'd have you covered before, during, and after your century training.) He has over fifteen years' experience coaching cyclists of all levels in most cycling disciplines, including road racing, mountain bike racing, century training, cyclocross, and BMX. Mike also manages and runs Team Revolution, based out of Revolutions Cycling Center. It includes over 175 road cyclists, triathletes, and mountain bikers of all levels.

Because people's skill levels vary, it is difficult to devise one training schedule that will fit every cyclist. So I asked Mike to put together a very basic, twenty-week training schedule that should work for most first-time cyclists. The schedule is definitely a good starting point when tackling century training, but keep in mind that a more specific training plan might be a better fit for you. The goal of your training is to prepare your particular body for your particular century ride. Getting a training plan made that specifically takes into consideration your body's strengths and weaknesses might end up being a lot more effective in the long run. For instance, if you are training for a particularly hilly century, you are going to need to work hills more than someone who is preparing for a flatter course. (You are also going to need to work your pain threshold a lot more, just FYI.)

If you are interested in a more specific schedule, ask your local cycle shop if it can recommend any good coaches in your area. Also, visit Mike online at www.revolutionscycling.com and www .berettapt.com to find out more about bicycle fitting, coaching, metabolic testing, and other cycling services. He can be reached at mike@revolutionscycling.com for cycling questions and schedules, or if you need another email address when you have to "forward this email on to ten people, and your dream will come true at 7:00 PM tonight." Mike is all about helping dreams come true—he's just that kind of guy.

Coach Mike's Notes

This is a twenty-week, gently progressing program designed for newbie cyclists who wish to complete their first century ride. It assumes that the rider could tolerate a fifteen-mile initial long ride. Riders who can't should gradually build up to the fifteen-mile distance and then begin the twenty-week program.

The program is based on three bike workouts each week (except for three weeks that require four rides). Riders can do more, but just make any additional rides *easy*. The column on the right is a good place to track your workouts. Simply put an X in the appropriate box after you complete a ride.

It's always best to train on your own bicycle, but sometimes circumstances can make that difficult. The long rides you do each week should be completed on your own bike. During the week, you can substitute spin classes, put your bike on a stationary trainer, or even use a bike at the gym (as a last resort).

Schedule Definitions

INTENSITY

How hard should you ride? A big goal in preparing for a century ride is learning how to use the gearing on your bike and keep your heart rate at a reasonable level. This process is unique for everyone, and some people will feel more comfortable pushing the intensity than others. Keep in mind that successfully completing your first century will be based on building up your "time in the saddle," so while intensity is important, more so is actually being on your bike, getting your body used to spending a lot of time on it. This training strategy may not lead to the fastest century you complete in your career, but you will finish!

For almost all your riding, use what's called the talk test: You should able to carry on a conversation while riding. If you're working too hard, your heart rate and breathing will be too high, and you won't be able to chat. Learn to use the gears on your bike to lessen the strain.

Ten weeks into the program, you will feel more comfortable pushing your limits, but for now, just get on the bike and ride!

RIDES 1 AND 2

These first rides will likely take place on weekdays and will be an hour or less in length, but they can be longer. At the beginning of the program, rides can be as little as twenty to thirty minutes long, and then should gradually progress in length up to one hour. Rides 1 and 2 can be completed on a stationary bike, on a trainer, and, of course, on the road. The emphasis of the workout and further details are listed below. A general guideline is given for the beginning number of repetitions, but everyone is unique. Set a goal for your initial workouts and then increase that goal as your training progresses. For example, on your first long-hills day, pick a hill or use a stationary trainer and decide how many times you will do the five-minute climb. After you complete the workout, record the specifics in your training log (see Appendix C). Next time you do a long-hill workout, look back at your records and add one to two reps to your previous workout.

FLAT AND STEADY

Pick terrain that is flat to rolling and maintain a steady intensity throughout the ride.

SHORT HILLS

Pick an appropriate hill for your fitness level, one that would take about one minute to climb. Start with five to ten one-minute repetitions. Recover as needed between reps. Add two reps to each session. This can be done on a stationary trainer or gym bike by increasing the bike's resistance. Use your gears to keep the pedals moving!

20-Week Training Program (Rider's First Century Ride)

	Ride 1	Ride 2	Ride 3
WEEK 1	Flat Steady	Long Hills	Long Ride
WEEK 2	Short Hills (Harder)	Flat Steady	Long Ride
WEEK 3	RECOVERY WEEK	1 Easy Ride During Week	Long Ride
WEEK 4	Long Hills	Flat	Long Ride
WEEK 5	Flat Steady	Long Hills	Long Ride
WEEK 6	Short Hills (Harder)	Flat	Ride Saturday and Sunday
WEEK 7	RECOVERY WEEK	1 Easy Ride During Week	Long Ride
WEEK 8	Hills	Flat	Long Ride
WEEK 9	Flat Steady	Long Hills	Long Ride
WEEK 10	Short Hills (Harder)	Flat	Ride Saturday and Sunday
WEEK 11	RECOVERY WEEK	1 Easy Ride During Week	Long Ride
WEEK 12	Long Hills	Flat	Long Ride
WEEK 13	Flat Steady	Hills	Long Ride
WEEK 14	Long Hills	Flat Steady	Ride Saturday and Sunday
WEEK 15	RECOVERY WEEK	1 Easy Ride During Week	Long Ride
WEEK 16	Long Hills	Flat	Long Ride
WEEK 17	Flat Steady	Hills	Long Ride
WEEK 18	Long Hills	Flat	Long Ride
WEEK 19	Taper	1 Easy Ride During Week	Long Ride
WEEK 20	Your First Century!	Flat Easy (1.5-2 hours)	

A BLANK TRAINING LOG IS AVAILABLE IN APPENDIX C TO HELP YOU TRACK YOUR PROGRESS.

LONG HILLS

Long hills are gradual to not-so–gradual hills that take longer than five minutes to climb. Start with as little as one rep during the first workout. Set a goal for your first ride and reach it. Pace yourself up long hills . . . steady the entire way. Don't poop out at the top! Add one to two reps each time you do a long–hill workout. These workouts can be done on a stationary trainer or gym bike by increasing the bike's resistance. Use the easier gears to keep your pedals moving!

20-Week Training Program (Rider's First Century Ride)					
	Length of Long Ride	Total Mileage for Week	Ride Completed		
WEEK 1	15	45			
WEEK 2	20	50			
WEEK 3	15	30			
WEEK 4	25	50			
WEEK 5	30	60			
WEEK 6	35	65			
WEEK 7	20	35			
WEEK 8	30	65			
WEEK 9	40	75			
WEEK 10	45	80			
WEEK 11	25	40			
WEEK 12	45	85			
WEEK 13	50	95			
WEEK 14	55	105			
WEEK 15	35	55			
WEEK 16	50	100			
WEEK 17	65	115			
WEEK 18	70	120			
WEEK 19	45	80			
WEEK 20	EVENT: 100 Miles				

A BLANK TRAINING LOG IS AVAILABLE IN APPENDIX C TO HELP YOU TRACK YOUR PROGRESS.

RIDE SATURDAY AND SUNDAY

Ride both days of the weekend; do the longer ride on Saturday. The length of the long ride is listed in the training log. Make the other ride half the length of the long ride. For example, if the long ride for that week is fifty miles, do that on Saturday and then ride twenty-five miles on Sunday.

Coach Dawn's Notes

This schedule and the training log in Appendix C are a great way to plan and track your training, but don't completely discredit my two-step century training program, either. It may sound like a joke, but sometimes just riding, and then riding some more, is a great way to train. Like Coach Mike says, the most important part of your training is just getting "saddle time," so even if you aren't feeling up to doing long hills or short hills or just-right hills, there is no reason why you can't still get some saddle time in.

Schedules are important because they give you structure, something to guide you along the way, and something to cross off when you've completed the day's assigned task. But they also give you something that glares at you as a constant reminder of all the sweating you still have left to do. If you are ever feeling overwhelmed or annoyed by your schedule and its demands, then I give you permission to just ignore it for a little while and focus on my two-step century training program. Forget about reps and intensity and athleticism and instead just hop on your bike and take it out for a spin. Go for a ride down to the 7-Eleven and get a Slurpee, or ride with your kid around the block a few times. Riding a bike can be a lot of fun, and as long as you can remind yourself of that throughout your training, you will continue to look at your bicycle as a good time, not a piece of metal sent to this earth to torture you and your unsuspecting muscles.

The Cycling

The expression "It's like riding a bike" is meant to convey that a particular activity is recalled easily, that our bodies naturally remember how to do it. Ironically, this expression doesn't apply to actually riding a bike—at least not riding a bike the correct way.

The last time a lot of us rode a bike, we were in junior high and there was someone on our handlebars. We spent most of the time on our bikes sprinting to the next location, standing up and pedaling hard, paying no attention to any sort of form or cadence. We weren't all that concerned with the various components of our bikes; we were just using them as the only form of transportation we had to get down to our best friend's house in time to catch our favorite show.

When you hop on your bike as an adult, it is important to treat riding as if it's a brand-new activity, something you have to learn to do. Yes, I understand that it feels like something you've done before, and that it therefore seems very easy to simply climb on the bike and ride off into the sunset. But what you have to remember is that (1) you are old now, and (2) you are riding a lot farther than down to your best friend's house. Because of (1), (2) is gonna hurt like hell if you don't ride your bike correctly. The good news is, once you retrain your brain to ride a bike like an athletic adult instead of a hyped-up kid, your new style will become second nature, just like the handlebar-balancing act was when you were eleven years old.

Following are a few major areas you are going to need to concentrate on in your cycling-relearning efforts. Work on them during your first few rides, and you'll be ready to add someone on your handlebars in no time.

Pedaling

It's instinct to hop on your bike and pedal hard, standing up occasionally, coasting after long sprints. This is not the way to pedal long distances, or as an adult (although I'm still a pretty big fan of the coasting). One of the biggest lessons I learned when I started riding was how fast my legs were supposed to be moving. I had always thought of cycling as a sport where your legs move at a relatively slow pace, with quite a bit of resistance from the pedals. When I started training, however, I was instructed that my legs should be moving much faster, with much less resistance. The words "less resistance" intrigued me, so I tried it out. The strategy alleviated pain in my knees, so I was immediately onboard.

Basically, you are going to want to be doing 80 to 100 revolutions per minute (rpm). This speed is called spinning, because your legs will be spinning like crazy. A revolution is one—you guessed it—revolution of your pedals. In order to figure out your rpm, count how many revolutions you do in twenty seconds, then multiply that by three. This number might be rather low when you first start training, so you should make 80 to 100 rpm your target goal.

It might take you a little while to get used to this speed, and initially you may be able to maintain it for only short periods of time before you'll have to slow down a bit. Spinning is easier on your muscles and also gives you a great cardiovascular workout—both good things—but your heart might not be completely up to the task right off the bat. That's okay. Just make sure you try spinning regularly throughout your first rides to build up your endurance for it. As your heart gets used to this newfound love of rapid extremity movement, maintaining this speed will become easier. At first it is going to feel like you are pedaling really fast for not much payoff, but in the long run this strategy is going to alleviate strain on your knees and muscles, and help you maintain your energy levels throughout long rides.

Remember, 80 to 100 rpm should feel relatively resistance-free. If it doesn't, you need to downshift your gears to limit the resistance. Spinning is meant to preserve your energy levels, and if you are trying to pedal that fast against great resistance, you aren't going to preserve so much as perish.

Another key element of pedaling is maintaining a clean, smooth revolution. Don't just concentrate on the downward part of the pedaling. Keep your legs moving in steady, equally distributed circles. Invest in some clipless pedals (see page 36), which actually clip your shoe to the pedal. This allows you to maximize all of your pedaling, including the upward motion of your revolution. If you aren't comfortable with clipless shoes, or just don't want to make another cycling purchase, you should at least put your feet in the little toe clips that are on most pedals. These can be a bit awkward to get in and out of, so proceed with caution when getting on and off the bike. But they will help you maximize your entire revolution, which will lead to happy spinning.

Gear Shifting

Figuring out when and how to shift your gears is going to lead to even happier spinning. It is going to be the single most important thing you do to ensure a good ride. It is amazing what a difference a couple gear shifts can make in your overall enjoyment of cycling.

Gears can get somewhat complicated, with some in the front, some in the back, shifting up for high and low, or down for low and high. And other such nonsense. I will do my best to explain them with only as much detail as you really need to know. Basically, your bike chain wraps around a round metal thing by your pedals and another circle thing by your back wheel. The round metal things by your pedals are called the chainrings, and there are usually two to three of them. They are bigger in size than the round metal things in the back, called cogs. There are usually three to ten cogs. If you multiply the number of chainrings you have by the number of cogs you have, you will determine how many gears your bike has. And you might also start to get really bored with this entire thing.

The gear shift on the left-hand side of your handlebars shifts your chain from one chainring to another, while the gear shift on your right-hand side moves the chain from one cog to another. Shifting your chainring will result in dramatic pedaling changes, while shifting the cogs makes a less noticeable difference. Personally, I usually leave my chainring alone and just shift my cogs. But the great thing about gears is that there are a ton of different options, and you've got plenty of time on your hands while riding to experiment with them and figure out which ones you like the most in different situations.

You can spend time learning that higher chainrings mean harder pedaling, while higher cogs mean easier pedaling, but you can also just pedal and fidget with your gears along the way. It's going to be nearly impossible to look down at your chainrings and cogs while you are riding, so it's best to just get to know the gears naturally. However, you do want to do this natural discovery on flat, open road. Do not save your experimentation for hills or uneven terrain. That could end poorly.

When you want to shift, make sure you continue pedaling, although not at full speed. You should feel the chain actually shift to the next cog or chainring and then settle into its new home. Its new home should be a quiet one, so if your chain is rattling or making any noise, try shifting again so that the chain can settle correctly into a cog or chainring.

Some refer to the lower gears as "granny gears," as if only grannies would use them. These people are idiots, and are most likely sore and cranky after long rides. Do not ever be hesitant or ashamed to use the lower (granny) gears. They are your friends (much like grannies themselves) and will save your legs and knees from the torture of tackling long rides in higher gears.

It is a good idea to learn how to reconnect your gear chain if it slips off during shifting or other pedaling. I've never had my chain slip off, but nearly everyone I've ever ridden with has, and it wasn't good times for them. For those who knew how to put the chain back on, the fix was quick and easy; for the others who didn't, it was quick and easy once they found someone who knew how to do it. This procedure is not terribly complicated. You basically just put the chain back onto the chainring and cog that it fell off of, then pedal (with your hand) slowly until it's back on.

This is definitely something that is learned most easily by doing it, so take the time to watch when you see someone else doing it, or ask your Bike Maintenance Dude to demonstrate. Also, because we are living in the information age, in which you can get a video of pretty much anything on the Internet (many things that you should never have video of, actually), I recommend going to YouTube and searching for "how to fix a bike chain that has fallen off." A few videos will pop up, giving you a good step-by-step guide to how to complete the task. Conveniently, some other videos popped up during my search as well: "How to Tweeze Nose Hair" and "How to Toilet Train Your Cat." So really, you might want to set aside a little bit of time before jumping on YouTube, since there are clearly a lot of things to learn.

Position

There are three different positions available to road cyclists (if you don't count my popular Passed Out on the Side of the Road position—and you really should, as I found myself in that position just as frequently as any other). Road bikes have drop handlebars that curve down and make a little U on either side of the handlebars, with the brakes usually found on the U. This provides for quite a bit of handlebar and a few options as to where to put your hands on those bars. You will most likely find one position you favor the most, but it's a good idea to vary between the different positions, allowing your body a break from the same form for hours at a time. Even the slightest change in position can alleviate some muscle aches and numbing that are in your new future (if they haven't started already).

The first riding position involves riding with your hands on top of the handlebars. This is probably the most natural position, because it is the one we favored during our entire childhoods. It is also the one that allows you to be the most upright, which is, at least initially, more comfortable than leaning over for hours. This position is a good one, but if you don't have brakes on your top handlebar, it can make quick stops difficult. Also, this position creates the most wind resistance, so it can slow down your ride in the long run, completely destroying your dreams of setting world records. I know, that's a lot to give up.

In the second position, you move your hands down the U of the handlebars and rest them on top of the brake levers, with your thumb on top and your fingers actually dropped down onto the brake levers. This position gives you quick access to the brakes and cuts down your wind resistance a little, which means you can go faster and stop quicker.

The last position puts your hands all the way down on the drop handlebars, on the bottom part of the U. A lot of super-serious riders ride like this because they are super serious and want to eliminate as much wind resistance as they can. The rest of us find this position a bit painful for long periods of time and have never really had strong feelings about wind either way. This is a decent position, but it will take some getting used to because it essentially folds you in half and leaves you bent over completely while engaging in an athletic activity.

Whatever position you choose, ride it in a relaxed way. Don't lock your elbows or grip the handlebars too hard. Cycling can be a bumpy sport, and it's important that you stay loose to absorb those bumps. Try not to stay in any one position for too long.

Give your muscles some diversity and allow them to shift around a bit throughout your ride. I'm not saying this will stave off all muscle pain (only an epidural of some sort will accomplish that task), but it will help you a little.

Cornering

Cornering on a bike can be tons of fun once you get past the *holy crap, I'm going to tip over and go skidding across the road* feeling you get when you lean into a sharp turn while balancing on two very tiny wheels. The only real way to conquer that initial fear is to simply tackle a bunch of turns until you get comfortable with them and no longer feel like your life is in danger each time you take one on.

The important thing to remember about turning on a bike is that you're actually using your body to turn, instead of your handlebars. Cornering on a bike is really about redistributing your weight, leaning to one side of your bike or the other, and in so doing causing the bike to turn. When you see a turn coming up, you want to take it as wide as you can without veering into traffic, or perhaps a tree on the other side of the road. Make your pedals identically parallel to the ground before the turn. For sharper turns, position your outside pedal down and your inside pedal up. Push on the outside pedal with your foot while you are in the turn, providing a little counterbalance to the leaning your body will be doing toward the inside pedal. Don't pedal through the turns, and try your hardest not to brake. If you do have to use your brakes, do so gently, because any sudden braking could screw up the precarious balancing act you have going on and send you on that much feared skid across the road.

Hills

Hills are the best of times and the worst of times for cyclists. They have grueling climbs and exhilarating descents. I'll give you one guess as to which one of those is the worst of times.

UPHILL

When you see a hill up ahead, try to get into a hill-worthy lower gear before you get to the climb. Sometimes newbies have the tendency to pedal hard in a higher gear leading up to an impending hill, trying to get good momentum going to help them sail up the incline. This isn't a bad strategy, but just make sure that you downshift while you're still on flat land. Attempting to change gears dramatically from high to low once you are on the hill isn't easy, nor is it good for your chain. In fact, it's a good way to pop the chain right off the bike.

That's not to say that once you are on the hill you can't switch to lower gears in an effort to keep your pedals moving. On treacherous hills, I've been known to keep trying to find a lower gear long after I've hit the lowest possible one. I somehow feel as if a new, lower option could magically appear, making my climb smooth and effortless. It never quite works out like that . . . but I digress.

If you are unable or forget to change gears before you hit the hill, you can zigzag slightly up the hill while you shift to a lower gear. This will alleviate a little bit of the resistance against the chain, making it easier and safer to change gears. However, if you aren't able to do this without avoiding traffic, I'd say it probably wouldn't make it safer at all, so be cautious before you start randomly zigging and zagging all over the road, please.

You can also use the zigzagging method if you are having a particularly difficult time on a hill. Zigging sideways across the path will mean you are climbing a slightly smaller incline and may provide just enough relief to get you up the hill. Unfortunately, once you add in the zagging, you're essentially making your climbing distance twice as long as it would be if you just went straight up, and that's less than fun. Another climbing option that some find useful is to stand up off your seat while pedaling, which puts your entire body weight behind each pedal revolution. I've found this to work well for short climbing sprints, but I've never been able to maintain it for long periods of time (not that I'm able to maintain *anything* remotely strenuous for long periods). Ultimately, your best option for successful climbing is to find a low pedaling gear, push your butt way back on your seat, and pull up on your handlebars with each revolution. It may not be the quickest of climbs, but it will be the one that gets you to the top without the aid of Life Flight.

You should also be aware of your breathing while you are climbing hills. One of my biggest problems with hills is that I always forget to breathe. One might suggest that this is actually the biggest problem you can have. When I'm tackling a huge incline, my arms pulling up on the handlebars, my legs pushing hard, I always find myself holding my breath. And then I find myself a little dizzy. I'm not sure if anyone else instinctively stops breathing when faced with athletic struggles, but if you do, try to make a concerted effort to take deep, steady breaths through-out your entire climb. This will fill your body with much-needed oxygen and help you maintain a steady breathing pattern during a not-so-steady time.

Finally, if you've tried the low gears, the zigging, the breathing, the standing, and the zagging, and you are still feeling as though you aren't going to survive a particular hill, there is no shame in simply hopping off the bike and pushing it up the rest of the damn way. I know it seems embarrassing, but personally, when I'm pedaling with all my might and literally moving more slowly than I would be if I were walking, I always take that as a sign that perhaps my feet's energies might be better spent touching the ground. Plus, once I get off the bike and start pushing, I've found that it's a lot easier to get out all the cuss words that I was having to keep inside while I struggled with my breathing and pedaling. And once the cuss words have an outlet, things always start looking up.

DOWNHILL

The first rule of riding downhill is to have fun. Sure, there are some basic safety considerations to keep in mind, but ultimately the downhills are the most fun you are going to have on your bike, made even more fun by the fact that they follow the bad times of climbing up the hill. As a newbie rider, do your best to enjoy every second of your descents. Try to enjoy the cool air hitting your face and the fact that you are traveling ridiculously fast without having to move a muscle. It's truly a thing of beauty.

I am a strong proponent of no pedaling during these glorious downhill rides, simply because it seems wrong to exert any energy at all when gravity has you pretty much covered. But if you insist on pedaling during your time of rest, make sure you shift up to a higher gear, because the low gear that you've been in for your uphill ride is going to leave your poor legs spinning all over the place during your descent.

The speeds of downhill riding can be a little scary when you are starting out, so if you feel the need to slow yourself down a bit, try to do so in a calm way. Any sudden or sharp movements while traveling at high speeds can cause some significant safety issues. First, use your body to slow yourself down by sitting up as straight as you can, providing wind resistance for your bullet bike. Also, if you want to use the brakes, do so gently and evenly, so as not to overbrake one wheel or the other. Sometimes when I was traveling down steep, scary hills, I'd find myself lightly clinching my brakes the entire time, trying to slow myself down and maintain control of the bike. Then one of my bike coaches said, "Be careful not to lean on your brakes for the entire descent— that causes friction, and over the course of the hill it can make the tire explode." After hearing the words "tire explode," I began implementing a safer braking strategy, which involved squeezing the brakes lightly every once in a while when I was starting to feel a little out of control.

Downhill rides are fun and rewarding, so soak them in. But at the same time, keep an eye out for anything that may prove hazardous up ahead on your route. It's easy to get lost in the relief and beauty of a downhill ride, which is okay, but try not to daydream too much, because you might miss the squirrel who has decided the bike lane would be a great place to nibble on a snack.

While all of these tips are going to help lead you to cycling glory, please don't forget that getting your bike fitted correctly to your body before you even start riding is going to help you far more than any of these techniques. If your bike isn't fitted correctly, you could be Lance Armstrong and you'd still struggle with your rides (well, maybe not Lance Armstrong, cause he's sort of a badass, but you get the point). Take the time when you are purchasing your bike to work with the Bike Dudes and their magic Bike Dude Tools to get it ready for your body. (No, they can't replace the seat with a recliner—I already asked.) Once you've gotten that taken care of, you are ready to tackle your first few rides and your new riding style. Remember, after a little while all of these tips and tricks will just become second nature (sorta like the cursing that just flies out of your mouth at mile 53), and you'll be an expert in no time. Don't worry, it'll be easy. Just like, ahem, riding a bike.

The Miles

Doing a century ride might seem quite intimidating at first. After all, one hundred miles is not a short distance, and you're actually supposed to cover it over the course of a single day. But then you'll look at your training schedule and realize that one hundred miles is nothing compared with the more than one thousand miles you'll be doing to prepare for the century. Not that I'm trying to get you freaked out about the training, but seriously, it's a lot of miles. Below are a few tips on how to make those miles a little less intimidating.

Where to Ride

OUTDOORS

You can ride your bike pretty much anywhere outside, which makes your training options pretty wide open. You can take off directly from your house, or you can drive to a local bike trail and get in some miles away from cars. I've always found that the rides that originate from my house seem to be the easiest to actually do. Leaving from and returning right to my garage saves me at least half an hour I would have spent loading up the car and driving to a trail. Keep these kinds of things in mind when you are planning your rides for the week. Sometimes saving that extra half hour can really help you out with your already tight work/life schedule.

It's difficult when you are training for a century ride to think of your bike as anything more than a chunk of hardware sent to annihilate you with butt and back pain. However, you should make an effort to seek out some fun times on your bike as well, so that it might actually have a shot of becoming a regular part of your life after your century ride is over. A big goal of your training should be to keep it interesting and fun. It's going to lose its luster pretty quickly if you are covering the same routes on all of your required rides.

The coolest thing about cycling is that it's a great way to find an adventure. In Chapter 3, "The Riding," I go into detail about the different riding that people do on their bikes, whether or not they are training for an event. Hop on your bike and head out for a day trip through a local park, cruise down to the grocery store, or maybe even ride to work one day.

INDOORS

The best place to train for a road race is always going to be on the actual road. I know, who woulda thought? But sometimes weather or time of day or agoraphobia keeps you from getting outside, and you still need to get your miles in. If this is the case, there are a few indoor-training options available to you.

Trainer

A bike trainer is a device that allows you to ride your road bike in place. (I'm a big fan of making that particular place in front of the TV, but that's just me.) A trainer holds the back tire of your bike in place and allows it to spin freely while you pedal. Using a trainer is a great way to get time on your actual bike when you can't get outside. It even offers a way to reduce and increase resistance so you can have a varying workout.

Exercise Bike

If you have an exercise bike in your home or at your local gym, it can be a great way to get some spinning in. These bikes range from simple to ridiculously complicated, with huge information panels blinking all sorts of exercise facts. Other than the entertainment value of lights and numbers, it doesn't really matter what kind of exercise bike you decide to use.

Just keep in mind that most exercise bikes are designed to have you sitting with your back almost completely vertical. This is an okay way to work your legs, which will aid your training efforts, but it in no way duplicates the form you will have on your actual road bike. And getting your back and neck used to that form should be a big part of your training, so try not to do too much of your riding on any bike that doesn't teach you the correct position.

Spin Classes

Most gyms and some community centers, like the YMCA, offer spin classes on a daily basis. These classes provide quick, difficult exercise and are a good way to get in a great workout and build the hell out of your leg muscles. Spin classes feel like cycling on crack, with their fast music and pace, as well as an instructor whose positive attitude and overall energy level are clearly indicative of drug use. If you often find yourself riding on the open road, thinking, *If only there were twenty more people here with me and some techno music playing, this ride would be perfect!* then spin classes might be just the thing for you.

All kidding aside, spin classes are a great way to kick your ass into cycling shape. They carry quite a bit of bang for your buck.

You could accomplish the same workout riding by yourself on your bike, but somehow the pressure of the other participants and a yelling instructor tends to be slightly more motivating than the pretty clouds and trees that surround you on your individual rides.

Each indoor option will require you to pedal the entire time—no coasting allowed. I know, it's hard to imagine cycling without coasting. It's my favorite part, too. Just keep in mind that you are going to tire out more quickly when you're not allowed to stop pedaling for the duration of your workout. Also, because you are riding nowhere quick, you are going to miss out on the cooling breeze that comes from being outside, which means you are going to get hotter quicker. These aren't bad things—just be aware of them so you can plan your indoor workouts to be a little shorter than your outdoor ones. (Or go ahead and just stop around the time your body and brain feel as though they may internally combust.)

While all three of the listed indoor options are good, remember that riding outside is always going to be your best bet for training. Even the most high-tech indoor options aren't going to be able to duplicate the feeling and requirements of riding outside. A big part of training for a long ride is training for the conditions of that ride and getting your body ready for them. Unless you are planning on doing the most boring century ride in the history of the planet, you are most likely going to be doing your race outside, so the more time you can train outside, the better.

How to Ride

There are a couple of general rules to proper cycling, ones that all newbies should know before they head out on their first ride.

WHERE YOU'RE SUPPOSED TO RIDE

In general, you are supposed to ride on the right side of the road, in the same direction as traffic, but make sure you don't hug that side too much. It's instinctive as a new rider to stay as far to the right as possible, for fear of getting hit by a very large car coming up behind you. However, that very large car needs to be aware of you and your bike, and by riding too far to the right, you risk the possibility of being unseen by motorists. In addition, hugging the right side of the road gives you little to no wiggle room should something go wrong and you need to maneuver quickly.

Make your presence known by riding a little out from the far-right-hand side, claiming your place on the road. If the road is too narrow for both you and a car to ride on side by side, fall in line behind the automobile as if you were a car yourself. In fact, instead of falling in line *behind* the car, perhaps you could just fall into the *back seat* of the car, making everything easier for everyone.

HAND SIGNALS

There are standard hand signals that all cyclists are supposed to use: Pointing left announces a left turn, and bending your left arm up at the elbow indicates a right turn. I'm a big fan of just pointing to the left or the right, depending on where I'm going—none of this bending-at-the-elbow nonsense. Also, to indicate that they are slowing down or stopping, cyclists are supposed to bend their left arm down at the elbow and point to the ground. This looks like someone in search of a "low five" every time I see it, so it begs the question of whether motorists will even have any clue what you're doing.

Hand Signals

Here is a breakdown of some of the hand signals you are going to need out there on the open road, and what they will mean to the other people on the road with you. Don't leave home without them (the signals or the people; you'll need *someone* to change your flat tires).

1. (Arm out and hand facing down) "I'm slowing/stopping."

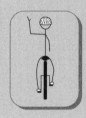

2. (Arm out and hand facing up) "I'm turning right."

>>>

3. (Arm straight out to the left)
"I'm turning left."

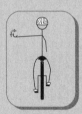

4. (Hand pointing at butt area)
"My ass hurts."

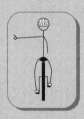

5. (Arm out, hand up and curved around
an imaginary wine glass, rotating wrist
up and down) "I need some booze."

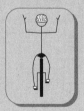

6. (Arm straight out, hand in hitchhiking
pose with thumb out) "Please,
somebody give me a ride in something
with an engine."

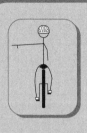

7. (Both arms out and hands facing up,
similar to the touchdown signal in
football) "I want to eat a pizza *thiiiiiis*
big. Right now."

>>>

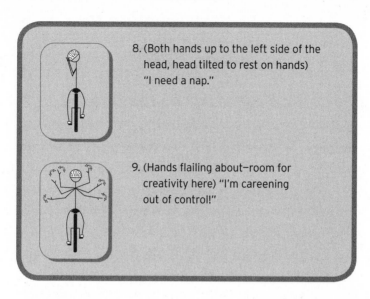

8. (Both hands up to the left side of the head, head tilted to rest on hands) "I need a nap."

9. (Hands flailing about—room for creativity here) "I'm careening out of control!"

Ultimately, most of the things you learn about bikes and riding are going to come from simply heading out on your bike, ride after ride. And you'll learn even faster if you make a point of riding with other cyclists. Experienced riders will have all sorts of tips and tricks that you can pick up during your time with them. Ask them questions and listen to what they have to say, but also do yourself a favor and ride behind them for part of each ride, making note of all the little things they do. This sounds somewhat stalkerish, but they've picked up these habits over the years and have already gone through trial and error and come out successful. Don't worry, you'll still have plenty of errors of your own to learn from, so you won't totally miss out on the joy that is the learning curve.

The Mind

So you're stuck on a bike for hours at a time. Hours of doing nothing but cycling and avoiding car bumpers. Think of all the deep thoughts you'll have! (Beyond simply *I'd really like to avoid the bumper of that car.*) With all that time, you will surely ponder all the deep thoughts of the day. And then, after those twenty-four seconds are over, you are going to need something to help you pass the time.

One way to occupy your brain during the hours it is going to spend staring blankly at the horizon, daydreaming about a warm bath and several ice packs (your brain doesn't care that those two don't mix so well), is using your iPod (or similar MP3ish device). Some may argue that it's not so safe to ride around town with headphones over your ears, effectively blocking all sounds that might prove helpful in those avoiding-the-bumper efforts we spoke of earlier. To those people I offer a compromise: Wear only one earpiece, on the ear that is not facing oncoming traffic. This will allow plenty of important sounds in, while at the same time providing some nice distraction sounds.

The great thing about an iPod is that you can theoretically change its contents before every ride, giving yourself new things to listen to every time. While there are definitely some things you won't mind listening to over and over again during your training, it's a good idea to keep things fresh and try your best to keep your mind on its toes with new audio treats on a regular basis. Anything that can prevent your training from feeling repetitive will go a long way in helping you want to repeat it, ironically enough.

Below, I've suggested some possibilities for filling your iPod, your training time, and your wandering mind.

Music

Your entire ride can be altered simply by your choice of music. It's a proven fact that with the right music, your ride can go from horrible to funky fresh in a matter of seconds. (And by "proven fact," I mean not proven by science so much as by an in-depth analysis of when a frown and/or smile appeared on my face while riding my bike around all of God's creation.)

While it's important to have a soundtrack to go along with your riding, it's not enough to hop on your bike with just any playlist. Oh, no, that plan could be disastrous. You must carefully examine and select the songs that will make it to your Cycling Mix, taking great pains to pick only the best and most upbeat ones. Ones that will move your legs with the sheer force of their rhythm and lyrics. Ones that will take you away, if only for a second, to a place where poetry and music intertwine around your soul and in your muscle tissue, inspiring them to reach for new heights. Throw some Sir Mix-a-Lot in there, too, because that man knows how to weave an inspiring lyrical tale. (Example: "Turn around. Stick it out. Even white boys got to shout.")

The following are some general music types that will make great additions to your Cycling Mix. I, for one, am a big fan of variety. I've heard something about it spicing up life, as well as training regimens. I recommend putting a wide variety of songs on your playlist so that you will have music to match the many moods you're going to be experiencing while training (ranging all the way from "ouch" to "holy crap, ouch"). After my detailed descriptions of each music type, I've allowed space for you to brainstorm some songs that you like in that particular genre. Use these notes to help you build your Ultimate Cycling Mix.

HIP-HOP

Hip-hop provides a great background beat for any athletic activity. If you find an infectious song, you just can't help but bounce to the rhythm. This bouncing can continue down to your legs and help lead you up a hill, or maybe through a difficult sprint. The only possible negative of hip-hop is that the songs tend to be a bit repetitive. If you are hovering anywhere near complete insanity from your workout, the repetition of an annoying hip-hop chorus might be just enough to push you over the edge. Proceed with caution.

Hip-hop songs to add to your playlist:

_____

_____

_____

_____

_____

TECHNO

Techno has all the wonderful features of hip-hop, as far as infectious beat goes, but also offers about 875 times as much repetition and $\frac{1}{574}$ as many actual words. Some people love to listen to techno music the entire time they are working out or riding. These people apparently haven't heard of all the difficult ramifications of having a stroke.

Techno songs to add to your playlist (as if you can actually
tell them apart):

_____

_____

_____

_____

_____

OLDIES BUT GOODIES

I grew up listening to my mom and dad's oldies stations, so hearing music from the '50s and '60s always makes me smile (then it
makes me frown because I remember that my parents didn't introduce me to modern music until I was thirteen—I never even had
a shot at being cool). Even if oldies music doesn't take you back
to your youth, it's still fun, and it does have a way of reminding
you of a simpler time. Simpler than the time you are having while
riding a bike for five hours—that much is for sure.

Oldies songs to add to your playlist:

_____

_____

_____

_____

_____

DEPRESSING LOVE SONGS

I'm sorry, but there is just something spectacular about a good
depressing love song (again, try not to be intimidated by my coolness). Belting out a heartbreaking song about love lost, found,

destroyed, or longed for can lift my spirits to new heights, if only because my muscle pain feels insignificant in comparison with such heartache.

Love songs to add to your playlist:

_____

_____

_____

_____

_____

COUNTRY SONGS (SLOW)

These songs would theoretically fall into the above category, but I feel like slow country songs take depression to an entirely different level than most soft rock. People are dying, children are crying, husbands are lying, and that's just the first verse. If the depressing love songs above aren't quite enough to make you feel good about your training, a slow country song will have no problem making your current situation seem downright merry by comparison.

Slow country songs to add to your playlist:

_____

_____

_____

_____

_____

COUNTRY SONGS (FAST)

A good fast country song can be just as infectious as a hip-hop song, with a catchy tune and fun beat. Granted, the stories being told in country songs are a little more boot-scootin' instead of gangbangin', but still, catch the right fast country song, and you'll have no choice but to get a little excited about the boozin', cruisin', and schmoozin' going on.

Fast country songs to add to your playlist:

_____

_____

_____

_____

ANGRY ROCK

A little bit of angry rock goes a long way—man, that little bit can really help you get out quite a bit of aggression. Sometimes you don't need a good beat or good lyrics or pretty instruments. Sometimes you need to hear someone screaming at the top of their lungs in a way that sounds as if their vocal chords may actually come flying out of their mouth in a violent protest against all that is wrong with the world. Sometimes this shrieking is the only possible musical representation of your inner thoughts and training turmoil. Be careful with this music, however. If you listen to too many angry rock songs, it will only be a matter of time before you are throwing your bike (repeatedly) at passing cyclists because the music has led you to a very dark place.

Angry rock songs to add to your playlist:

_____

_____

_____

_____

INDIE ROCK

Indie rock is often introspective and deep. It takes the world, turns it around in the palm of its hand, and then writes a poem to music about what it has gleaned. (There is also usually a large bong involved in some capacity during that progression of events.) You, too, may become introspective while you are training, as physical exhaustion often leads to deep and/or homicidal thoughts. Indie rock may prove to be the perfect companion to your elevated state of awareness and depth (and I wouldn't rule out the large bong, either).

Indie rock songs to add to your playlist:

_____

_____

_____

_____

BROADWAY

Who doesn't love a little Broadway music? I mean, besides most straight men, children, many women, and some animals? I may be in the minority with my ridiculous affection for Broadway music, but if you happen to be as big a dork as I am, then throw the entire score of your favorite show on your iPod and you'll feel like you are spending your time in a Broadway theater, instead of out on the road. You may, however, wonder when theater seats got so uncomfortable. . . .

Broadway songs to add to your playlist:

_____

_____

_____

_____

_____

Books on Tape

In addition to standard music MP3s, I also highly recommend listening to some books on tape while you are riding. They will hold your attention much better than music and will also help you avoid all that pesky reading that is usually involved in digesting books. Below, I've listed a few ideas to help you pick out some good books to help pass your training time. I've allowed space here as well, so that you can list some possible books on tape to add to your training mix.

HUMOR BOOKS

Let's be honest: Not much is going to seem all that humorous while you are riding up a ninety-degree incline and being passed by disabled seniors using walkers (although that scenario will seem quite humorous to everyone who hears the story—you might even consider writing a book about it . . . ahem). Humorous books, whether they are essay collections or novels, are a great way to bring a little levity to some very nonhumorous training moments, and they can help keep your sense of humor intact when it could very easily disappear into a blur of curse words and sweat.

Possible humor books to listen to:

_____

_____

_____

DEPRESSING MEMOIRS

On the other hand, why do you want to hear fun, jovial stories while you are suffering such great pain? You know what you really need? A story of someone whose pain was much greater than yours. This will give you a little perspective and make you realize that people have overcome a lot more than a silly ninety-degree hill. The more depressing the story, the better—you are going to need a lot of perspective.

Possible depressing memoirs to listen to:

_____

_____

_____

TRAVEL BOOKS

Sure, you are only riding around your neighborhood, but why can't you learn all about the wonders of faraway lands at the same time? Imagine you are cycling through those lands, instead of through a strip mall downtown. If you squint a little, that mini-mart up ahead might look a little like Mayan ruins. . . .

Possible travel books to listen to:

_____

_____

_____

COOKING BOOKS

This suggestion could be either great motivation or horrible torture; I'm not sure how it will work out for you. While you are burning millions of calories pedaling away, you can hear tales of how to create some amazing food to replace all of those calories. Maybe you can even swing by the store on your bike and pick up the ingredients so you can enjoy a reward meal when you get home. That could be awesome. Or, if you are like me and can barely make microwave mac 'n' cheese, cooking books could just be a reminder of all the amazing food you will never prepare for yourself. In that case, skip the grocery store and find a good restaurant to stop at instead.

Possible cooking books to listen to:

_____

_____

_____

MY BOOK

You could always listen to this very book while you are riding yourself silly. Or perhaps my first book, *The NonRunner's Marathon Guide for Women*. Both are great exercise companions, although—and this could be a bit of an issue—they aren't available on tape. So you're going to need to somehow create a device that holds the books out in front of you while you are riding. Or have someone ride beside you and read them to you while you ride! Either way, I don't see how this won't turn out well.

Possible people who can ride beside you and read my book(s) to you:

_____

_____

_____

LANGUAGE TAPES

Technically, these aren't books on tape, but being trapped for hours with nowhere to go is a great time to learn a new language. Not only will you be working toward becoming a cycling god(dess), but you will also be able to watch Telemundo by the end of your training. Think how much better those Spanish soap operas will be when you actually understand what they're saying.

Possible languages to learn:

_____

_____

_____

While I highly recommend loading up your iPod for your training, make sure to be cautious when you are listening to it. In some situations, wearing even one headphone is going to be way too distracting. I spent a week riding through the beautiful countryside in Switzerland and never went long without my headphone attached to my right ear. But when I was riding around New York City on a bike, I never even thought of putting a headphone on (mostly because the only thing I actually thought of during that entire ride was *Eeeeeeeeeeek, cars!!!!!*).

Listen to your instincts and your comfort level and let those two things help you decide whether the iPod is a good idea for each particular ride and location. Trust me, you do not want to be the jackass who is riding around oblivious to your surroundings. You will not only be annoying the other people (motorists and cyclists) on the road with you, you'll be putting them at risk, too. And by "putting them at risk," I mean you will be motivating them to run into you with their car or bike, which will in turn be putting them at risk of being convicted of aggravated assault with a large metal object. Good news is, that sounds like the beginning of a great country song that might one day make its way to your playlist, bringing the whole thing full circle.

The Body

W hen your mind comes up with the great idea to tackle a ridiculous physical challenge like a century ride, it's your body that ends up paying the price. Leg muscles that used to flex only when pushing the footrest of the recliner down are now being made to spin around in circles for hours at a time. Arms that haven't lifted anything heavier than a Snickers ice cream bar in two years are now being asked to support your upper body as you lean on the handlebars of your bike. Your butt muscles— well, their trauma is just too much to even put into words. You'd think that the butt would have been prepared for all of the sitting required of cyclists, seeing as sitting used to be your favorite pastime. But you're so very wrong.

Since you are throwing your poor, innocent body to the wolves with your physical ambitions, the least you can do is help it out a little bit. Below I've listed out some things to consider when attempting to keep your body in functioning order for the duration of your training. (Following your training, the only function that will be in order will involve the difficult napping-while-eating-ice-cream combo.)

Food

One of the greatest things about getting off your butt (or rather, off and then on again) and actually burning calories is that you get to replace those calories with food once you're done with the exercising. In fact, you *must* replace those calories with food or your body will grow very weak and perish. And if you are going to perish while training for a century ride, it should at least be in some dramatic way, like being attacked by a mountain lion, or perhaps an out-of-control crotch fire that started after you forgot to apply your Butt Butter before a long ride.

During your training you will take on levels of hunger that you never knew existed. All-you-can-eat buffets start seeming like a perfectly logical choice for every meal, because while the rest of your body is getting smaller from all your exercise, your stomach seems to be growing by the day. While it is tempting to fill this growing stomach with anything and everything in your sight line, you really should do your best to eat well while you are training. Apparently, nutrients and things like vegetables (not the tempura kind) actually go a long way in helping you not only survive, but also thrive, during your training. I know, I was heartbroken about this scientific discovery, too.

In addition to just generally eating healthy and being a nutritious superstar, you are going to need to incorporate more carbohydrates than normal into your diet—so not all is lost. There are two kinds of carbs: simple and complex. Simple carbs are found in fun things that contain sugary goodness, like cookies, ice cream, and pretty much anything else you love eating. But these are not what you want to be going for. You should instead be concentrating on complex carbohydrates, the ones that are found in foods like pasta, bread, fruits, and vegetables. These foods are going to have fiber and carbs and other great nutrients your body needs. They are also going to break down slower, providing your body with a steady stream of energy instead of the quick spike of energy that the sugary carbs deliver (I love that spike most of all). When you are looking for complex carbs, you are going to want to keep an eye out for whole wheat as an ingredient, instead of flour. Basically, the fewer processed carbs, the better, which sorta seems like an oxymoron to me. Who knew carbs came unprocessed?

In general, you want carbs to make up about 65 percent of your daily food intake. However, if you are taking in that amount and are still not feeling like a ball full of energy, then you should probably start eating even more carbs. Some cyclists eat five hundred grams of carbohydrates every day, but I'm thinking that they don't incorporate quite as much coasting as I do in my rides.

Protein is also an important part of your diet, because it helps build and maintain muscle and other body tissue. But cyclists don't necessarily have to eat any more protein than the average healthy person; it's just important to actually eat proteins, because sometimes they can be the easiest thing to forget. Meat, fish, eggs, dairy, beans, and nuts are all sources of protein and should make up about 15 percent of your daily food intake.

BEFORE, DURING, AND AFTER YOUR RIDE

While you need to eat well all day long, it is also extremely important to eat well just before, during, and just after your rides. This will help you maintain a high enough energy level to support your ridiculous body movement. A big part of your training is experimenting with different pre-, during-, and postride foods to figure out which ones work for you and are agreeable to your stomach. I found that cycling traumatized my poor stomach much less than high-impact sports do, which means I can eat more food more frequently while I train, without fear of digestive rebellion. This opens up your eating options considerably.

Your food intake during your ride will make or break your attempts at cycling. If you don't take in enough food, your journey to the finish line is going to be an ugly one. Your muscles are fueled by glucose, and your body can store only enough to keep you upright for about ninety minutes' worth of moderate exercise. This is why you have never in your life actually run out of glucose reserves, because channel hopping does not fall into the moderate-exercise column. Unfortunately for you, your new sport is a long-distance one and will require you to refuel your body as you are riding.

Carbohydrates are the quickest and most efficient way to get glucose to your muscles. There are many options for cyclists when it comes to carbs. You can go the energy bar/gel route and eat products specifically made for exercising, or you can bring your own treats along. This is really a matter of personal taste. Some people cannot stand the taste of energy bars or gels. These people aren't likely to be overly enthusiastic about ingesting them while they are riding. If you are one of these people, it might be better for you to bring along some snacks that aren't cycling-specific, such as crackers, sliced-up peanut butter sandwiches, mini-muffins, dried fruit, or dry cereal. All of these can be carried in a plastic baggie and grabbed easily while you are riding, or eaten during a rest (nap) stop.

The most important thing about eating during your ride is doing so *before* you feel hungry. Once you feel hungry, you will be running on fumes (literally, if you are riding in a high-traffic area) and fighting an uphill battle to replenish your depleted reserves. And you have enough uphill battles to worry about already. Keep track of how long you have ridden, and take in a snack at least every twenty to thirty minutes along your ride.

You are also going to want to eat thirty minutes before and within the thirty minutes following your rides to help provide some energy for the ride and replace the energy you burned during it. The postride food is probably more important, as it will have the greatest effect on how you feel the next day. You might not be in the mood to stuff your face right after a ride, but it's really important, so do your best to take in as much as you can manage.

There are also several "recovery" drinks out there on the market that have gained popularity recently. Much like Gatorade is supposed to aid your athletic performance, recovery drinks are meant to aid your postperformance. They are good alternatives to eating actual food, simply because you might be more likely to gulp down a drink than to chomp on food right after a hard workout.

DRINK

Water is your friend all the time, but especially around the time you jump into sweat-happy activities. Dehydration, on the other hand, is not a friend at all, and it should be a very large goal of yours to avoid meeting him. The best way to accomplish this task is to make sure you are taking in plenty of fluids when you are out on your bike. You should be drinking at least four ounces of liquids every fifteen minutes, even more if you have chosen to move around in hot weather.

In addition to (or in place of) water, you should take a sports drink along on your rides. It will provide you with hydration and hit you with a replenishment of electrolytes, sodium, carbohydrates, and other helpful nutrients that your body is expelling in protest of this whole body-movement kick you're on.

As with eating, it's important to drink long before you feel any sort of thirst kicking in. Try to get yourself on a schedule, or perhaps set your watch so you don't accidentally go an hour and a half without taking a drink.

Also, if you are a fan, coffee or other caffeinated beverages can put a little pep in your spin if you drink one an hour or two before your ride. Just be careful not to drink too much in an effort to turn yourself into a Speedy Gonzalez/Tasmanian Devil hybrid. At a certain point, too much caffeine will react poorly with your stomach and probably leave your brain a little fried as well.

Stretches

There are roughly 896,745 stretches that can be done to aid cyclists and their muscles. There are entire books and websites devoted to stretching, and you might want to consult some of those for ideas aplenty regarding your stretching options. You should also ask other cyclists what stretches are their favorites and try some of those out. Most important are the stretches that help your back and legs, with a couple thrown in for your neck. You will be in a new and uncomfortable position when riding, bent over at the waist with your head tilted up. Add this to all that pedaling, and you're going to have quite a few muscles in need of a little relief.

I've illustrated a few cycling stretches I'm fond of and how you can practice for them during your time out of the saddle. Please note that I even added a little butt padding to my cycling stretcher guy, as I'm trying to do my best to prepare you for that visual.

>>>

1. CYCLING STRETCH

Pull your ankle up toward your butt, keeping your knees together and hips aligned, and stretch out your quadriceps.

1. REAL-LIFE STRETCH

You know that dance from the '90s, the one where you grab your ankle and pull your leg back repeatedly to the beat of "Ice Ice Baby"? This stretch is sorta like that dance, if it were done *really* slow. Practice at home to your favorite slow song. (White man's overbite required for effective execution of this dance.)

2. CYCLING STRETCH

Put your foot out in front of you and roll it around in circles, stretching out your ankle.

2. REAL-LIFE STRETCH

Next time you drop a piece of food on the floor in the kitchen and you want your dog to eat it so you don't have to bend over and pick it up yourself, go ahead and incorporate a little spin in that foot you are using to point.

>>>

3. CYCLING STRETCH

Roll your head back and forth and around slowly in circles, working out the muscles in your strained neck.

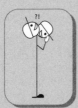

3. REAL-LIFE STRETCH

You won't actually be practicing this stretch yourself in your day-to-day life, but you will have a firsthand look at it in action every time you tell someone you are training for a one-hundred-mile bike ride. Their eruption of laughter will cause their head to bounce back and forth and possibly spin around in circles.

4. CYCLING STRETCH

Lie on your back and pull your knees up to your chest to stretch out your lower back.

4. REAL-LIFE STRETCH

You will most likely be practicing this particular stretch pretty much every night following a long ride. It might be the only position you're able to be in, because of your sore legs, neck, and butt muscles. As an added bonus, you may actually need to sleep like this, too.

>>>

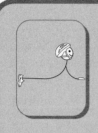

5. CYCLING STRETCH

Lie down on your stomach, then push your upper body up off the ground, stretching out your back.

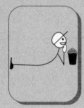

5. REAL-LIFE STRETCH

You won't be pushing so much as stuffing when you practice this stretch at home while lying in front of the TV, eating popcorn. Feel the burn?

Getting on the Bike

Now that I've actually purchased a bike, one would assume that I've made a very large step in the direction of actually beginning my training. But then again, one should know better than to make rash assumptions about me and movement. It turns out that merely putting a shiny new bike in your garage (with matching shiny helmet) does not a training plan make. Apparently, an even larger training step involves my actually getting *on* the bike. And then it would really help if I pedaled. At least a little bit. Because it turns out that coasting is not nearly as big a part of cycling as I'd hoped. Hmph. Why does everything have to be so complicated?

My thirteen-year-old cousin, Katy, went with me when I purchased my shiny bike. Since that time, she has repeatedly grilled me about whether I've gone riding. To which I always reply, "Yes, I have." To which she, in a line of questioning I feel is a bit intrusive, not to mention untrusting of her elder, snips, "I mean other than the two minutes you rode it around the parking lot at the bike store." At which point I threaten to use the bike to inflict harm on her the next time I see her. "Well, at least then you'd be doing *something* with it." It's hard to imagine where this child learned such sarcasm.

I'm not exactly sure why I haven't gotten on the bike. I mean, it sits there in the garage, mocking me with its shininess every time I see it. You'd think I'd eventually give in and take it out for a spin. But, again, you'd be grossly underestimating my ability to put off any sort of sweat-inducing activity. It's a skill I've honed for many years; I wouldn't expect you to understand.

>>>

>>>

I've been trying to come up with different ways to get myself into the training mindset. How do I inspire myself to once again put on athletic shoes and head out into the world of ridiculously high heart rates and dangerously tight athletic shorts? I was running a little low on inspiration, so I decided I'd just go with good old ingenuity.

My main stumbling block with getting on the bike is trying to fit the biking into an already busy schedule. I mean, I've got work and friends and family. And TiVo. Those things take up a lot of time. My TiVo alone can hold 150 hours of programming, leaving very little time for anything else. So I did what any good athletic warrior would do: I figured out a way to incorporate my TiVo into my cycling.

I went on Craigslist and searched for used exercise bikes. With every picture and exciting product feature, I grew more inspired. This would be awesome. I would buy one of these bikes at a drastically reduced price, and in no time I'd be spending hours upon hours pedaling away in the comfort of my own home. I'd enter information into the handy display panel, and in return it would enlighten me with tales of rpm, heart rates, and many other numbers that I would never fully understand or pay attention to. All the while, I would be watching my favorite TV shows, which would make me completely oblivious to the physical activity and the inevitable butt soreness. Again, this was all sounding quite awesome.

I found a pretty good bike for a pretty cheap price, and I went over to a pretty scary house to pick it up. When I arrived, the bike was sitting in the man's garage, the universally accepted dumping ground for all of our exercise hopes and dreams. Apparently, this man's dream had died some

>>>

>>>

time ago, because his bike was covered in a good three layers of dormant dust. He was nice enough to clean off the seat before I hopped on and took the bike for a test spin. The pedals went around in circles and the lights on the display panel lit up, so I was sold.

I loaded the bike into the back of my car, quietly judging this slightly pudgy man for never using his exercise equipment. Some people. Why buy something if you're never going to use it? I mean, really.

Katy came over the other day and saw the newest member of my family-room decor, pointed straight at the TV.

"Why is there a bike in here?"

"I thought if I put it right in front of the TV, I'd have no excuse for not riding."

"So, have you ridden this one?"

"Well . . . "

"Uh-huh."

"I did burn a lot of calories getting it up the stairs."

"What day of the training plan was that?"

Whatever.

The First Ride — Take 1

After weeks (that added up to months) of adhering to a strict Noncycling Cycling program, I was finally ready to head out on my first real bike ride. I would put on all my fancy cycling clothes, lace up my not-so-fancy running shoes, and take the shiny new bike on its inaugural roll. I called up my friend Sarah and asked if she would like to join me on this historic ride, the beginning of my cycling glory. "You're just now taking your bike out for the first time?" Sarah didn't understand that sometimes people must take their time with glory, not rush it.

Unfortunately, I was forced to take even more time before capturing the glory, because the day Sarah and I were supposed to meet I went to my garage, ready to embrace my long-neglected bike, only to find that it had expressed its hurt feelings by letting all the air out of its tires. I had to cancel on Sarah because I was convinced that there was some sort of defect with my tires.

Let me take a moment to briefly describe my relationship with tires. It is not a good relationship, to say the least. I have what I call bad tire karma. I don't know what I did or whom I did it to, but in this life I have been cursed with horrendously bad tire luck. I've had more than fifteen flat tires on my cars over the years. Once I had two in one day. Three times they've exploded on the freeway while I was traveling at rather high speeds. When I was younger I assumed I was just buying cheap, bad tires, but as I got older and started buying good tires, I came to realize that this karma had nothing to do with tire quality and everything to do with the universe

>>>

needing somebody to test how far one can drive on a rim of a tire. (My studies have found that rims are surprisingly sturdy and actually become even more so the higher the speeds— that is, if you're not bothered by sparks coming out of the bottom of your automobile.)

Needless to say, I was a little apprehensive when deciding to take on a sport that revolves around two tires and no airbag. When I came downstairs to find both tires flat on the day of my first ride, I was freaked out. I went to the bike store and bought a little hand pump so that I could refill my defeated tires. But when I got the pump home and actually looked at the tires, I discovered that the valve didn't look like anything I'd seen before, and that no matter how many times I put the pump on the valve, absolutely none of the air coming out of the pump was actually getting into the tire.

When I went back upstairs, I had a supportive voicemail from Sarah: "You better figure out what is wrong with your tires, because I don't feel like getting stuck out there with your flat tires. My bike is pretty cool, but I don't think it could balance me, you, and your bike on it. I'll be forced to leave you out there on the trail."

Not wanting to be left for dead on a bike trail, I took the bike in, ready for the Bike Dude to give me horrible news, ready to have to replace both tires, hopefully with some sort of impenetrable metal compound. But when I explained my flat tires and horrible tire karma to the Bike Dude, he just looked at me blankly and asked, "When was the last time you rode the bike?" Does *everyone* know I'm a cyclist who never actually rides her bike?

"It's been a while," I answered.

>>>

"Tires go flat after sitting for a while," he said, clearly not as traumatized by my flat tires as I was. "You just need to fill them up and you'll be fine. Do you have a pump?" I nodded and told him I had a hand pump that made air, but just couldn't quite get the air into the tire. He leaned over and unscrewed the top of my tire's valve. "Did you do that first?" Hmmm.

Now that I had officially identified myself as the stupidest noncycling cyclist on the planet, the Bike Dude began showing me the store's collection of floor pumps. These things, standing at two and a half feet, put my little hand pump to shame. They had handles and gauges and places to put your feet. I wouldn't have been surprised if they'd filled up my tires all on their own.

Sadly, that didn't happen; instead, the Bike Dude showed me how to use the pump to fill my tires. He demonstrated how the pumping was done and then stepped aside to let me have a crack at it. It never fails to amaze me how completely useless my upper body is. When he was using the pump, he did it with an ease that made it seem like he could have done it with the strength of just his pinky finger. When I took over the pumping, it felt like I was pushing against a brick wall every time I pushed down. At first I thought my participation in this pumping was merely so I could get an idea of how the pump worked, and then he would clearly see that I was struggling and take over after I managed to push down once or twice. But as I was pumping away, pulling up and pushing down pathetically, practically lifting my feet off the ground in an effort to put some of my lower body into the pump, Bike Dude actually walked away from me. At that point it became

>>>

clear that I was meant to actually learn from this experience, and that he was therefore going to make me do all of the pumping myself. Pfft. Men.

I'd be pushing with all my might, nearly sitting on the pump, when he'd come by and look at the gauge. "Am I done?" I'd ask. He'd point to a much higher number on the gauge. "Not until you get up to this number." It was then that I became slightly worried about my athletic prowess and prospects, because I was actually winded and sweating from just the pumping up of my tires. I'm no fitness expert, but I'd have to say that this did not bode well for my ability to take on a one-hundred-mile bike ride.

The First Ride—Take 2

After my first attempt at my first ride was derailed by deflated tires, I rescheduled with Sarah. On our set day, I arrived at her house full of air and general excitement about cycling.

We made it four blocks from her house before our first stop: a cycle shop where we both hoped to stock up on some last-minute additions to our bikes. We wouldn't want to rush into this ride, you know? I'd already put it off for months, so what was a few more minutes, really? And the two of us had some very important things that needed to be attended to. Sarah needed a water-bottle holder, and I . . . well, I needed a kickstand. Sarah's need didn't inspire a mocking look from Bike Dude, just so you know.

"A kickstand?" Bike Dude asked.

"Yeah, for some reason my bike doesn't have one."

"That's because road bikes don't have kickstands."

"Can you put one on?" The blank stare that followed seemed to imply that I was speaking a foreign language while vomiting on Bike Dude's shoes.

Apparently, road bikes don't have kickstands, and aren't meant to have kickstands, and will be made fun of if they have kickstands. This makes no sense to me. How the hell do you make a bike without a kickstand? Are you wanting it to fall over? I don't get it. And why is it uncool to want your bike to stay upright? I'm sure there is some mechanical or scientific or maybe just cosmetic explanation of the anti-kickstand movement, but their arguments fall on my deaf, balance-loving ears.

Once our modifications were (grudgingly) done, Sarah and I headed out to the nearby bike path and started out on my road to a century ride. Several things made me realize that this road wasn't going to be a smooth one. First of all, my ass started hurting approximately 4.2 seconds into the ride. It seems that harder seats are supposed to make for less butt pain, but surprisingly enough, putting a rock between my legs for the sake of sport doesn't exactly feel good.

You'd think my ass would have been somewhat protected by the Depends diaper that had been sewn into the seat of my spandex cycling shorts, but you'd be wrong. Almost as wrong as it is to send people out in public with butt pads and then ask that they get on a bike, bend over, and stick that butt out for the world to see. It's just all sorts of unfortunate.

But at least I wasn't alone while sticking my sore, padded butt in the air. Sarah rode beside me and listened to me complain in great detail about the various indecencies occurring around my arse. And it was actually nice to have someone with me. This surprised me most of all.

When I was training for my marathon, I had a ridiculously chipper friend, Jen, who trained with me. She loved loved loved chatting and loved loved loved running, so she was practically beside herself when given the opportunity to combine the two. On the other hand, I am not a huge fan of chatting or running, and, more than that, I'm just not capable of combining the two.

I can basically either run and breathe or talk and breathe. But I can't run *and* talk *and* breathe all at the same time. It was a trifecta I never quite mastered.

But as Sarah and I got into our ride, I realized that I was actually engaging in athletic activity *and* conversation at the same time. It was somewhat of a miracle, really, and definitely the first time such an event had occurred in my life.

Another miracle was occurring as well. I was actually doing something athletic and not feeling as though I might perish at any moment. Granted, we were hardly pushing ourselves to the extreme, but in general we were moving ourselves along at a decent pace and I wasn't feeling as though I might vomit. Which is usually my general disposition when participating in anything calorie-burning—it's a visceral reaction, really.

These good times and antinausea feelings began to fade in the second half of our ride, however. I didn't know why, but all of a sudden, as we headed back toward where we'd started, the pedaling got harder and I felt like the vomit feeling might eventually make an appearance. Shortly after I began preparing myself for my inevitable disdain and frustration toward cycling, I heard Sarah yell, "Aw, crap!" I looked back to see her pointing at my tire. "Your damn tire is flat. Crap, crap, crap."

This wasn't good news, per se, since my bike was malfunctioning. On the other hand, that was probably the reason it was so difficult to pedal. So maybe I didn't hate cycling after all!

Sarah didn't share my enthusiasm for my flat tire, needless to say. I got off my bike and looked at the tire while she rode around on her bike, circling me. I started pushing the bike, and she started riding as slowly as humanly possible on her bike. "What are you doing? Why don't you just get off your bike and push it, instead of trying to ride that slow?"

"Because! I'm not the one who has a flat tire! I don't have to push my bike! I told you not to get a flat tire!"

"Oh, did you? I totally forgot. If I had remembered, I wouldn't have gotten this flat."

After several more minutes of friendly conversation and doing the math on how many miles we were going to have to walk/roll slowly, we were able to flag down a nice man and his wife as they passed us on their bikes. They didn't look like they really wanted to stop, but we looked like we really needed them to stop, so they did. I knew these two could help us, because they appeared as though they'd been ripped out of the pages of a cycling magazine. From head to toe, they had everything any cyclist could want. Most important for me, they had a hand pump that fit my tire valve.

Much like the Bike Dude who showed me the floor bike pumps in the store, this guy was also a big fan of my learning how to use his pump, instead of his just pumping for me. Does everything have to be a lesson with these bike people?

Eventually, impatience won out over lesson time and the man grabbed the pump to finish the tire himself. He could see that with my weak arms, there was a good chance he was going to be there for the better part of the afternoon for the sake of my educational experience.

With my tire once again full, Sarah and I were able to finish the rest of the ride without much fanfare. Butt pain, yes. Fanfare, no.

So, if you're keeping score at home, that's one ride and one flat tire. Do you think AAA services bikes as well as cars? I should really look into that.

Passing the Time

I am a couple months into this biking thing, and overall it is going well. I have no major injuries to report, other than my legs' being covered in bruises that are actually starting to draw stares of concern. (I simply say, "I've been beaten by a piece of metal" when people inquire or stare too long.)

My biggest problem with this sport, like so many other sports, is the lack of entertainment it provides for my mind. I always have high hopes of solving all of life's questions and problems during the course of my riding, with plenty of time to take on world issues as well. But that just never happens. Sure, I have some thoughts, but most of them are of the *man, am I bored* variety.

So I've been forced to come up with other things to entertain my mind while I'm riding. Since I can't strap a TV to the bike (not yet, at least—I still hold out hope for the invention of the handlebar screen), my only entertainment comes via my iPod. Even then, the five million songs I have on my iPod have a way of boring me with their predictability. I mean, I put them all on there, so of course I'm not surprised when one starts playing.

Recently I've started listening to downloaded podcasts of my favorite talk radio shows. *The Adam Carolla Show* and *Frosty, Heidi and Frank* have, on several occasions, prevented my eyes from glazing over, which would surely have sent my bike careening off the road and into a tree and/or pedestrian. Unlike music, which has a way of fading into my subconscious, becoming mere background noise as I fall deeper into a boredom-induced coma, talk radio forces you to really listen because people are having actual conversations. This is an activity that forces my mind to think of things other than the fact that I'm riding a bike for hours at a time with no hope of stopping anytime soon.

The talk radio shows I listen to are not only engaging, but funny as well. It's not unusual for me to be out riding by myself and burst into laughter at something on one of my podcasts. Sure, I get weird looks, but the good news is that if I'm riding downtown, I'm very rarely the only crazy person laughing at herself. So I fit right in.

>>>

Another iPod wonder I've become obsessed with are books on tape (or books on iPod, as it were). I feel so friggin' highbrow when I am exercising and "reading" at the same time. Look at me, all well rounded and whatnot. The first book I listened to was, appropriately, *It's Not About the Bike*, by Lance Armstrong. Lance had cancer and still managed to love riding his bike, so he inspired me to at least try to ride with a positive attitude. (Unlike Lance, though, I feel like it *is* about the bike for me, since the bike is what is causing the butt pain.)

The next book I downloaded was Anderson Cooper's *Dispatches from the Edge*. I love me some Anderson Cooper, and I'd heard a lot of good things about his book. He narrates the audio version himself, lending a personal touch to an already extremely personal story. The book weaves in and out of his past heartache and his experiences in places like Iraq and New Orleans following Katrina. It is a super-depressing book that makes me grateful that the only pain I have in my life right now involves an unfortunate bike rash. As I listened to Anderson talking about his brother's suicide and the many war-torn countries he's visited, I realized maybe I should just stop my bitching and ride in rashy-ass peace.

A Secret

I have a secret to share with you. It's a biggie, too. It turns out I don't totally hate this biking thing. Shhh, don't tell anyone; it would ruin my reputation. I'm not really sure why I don't despise cycling. I mean, it has all the ingredients of a crap sandwich (moving + sweating + effort - my TV = crap sandwich), yet remarkably, I find myself actually smiling while I'm pedaling along. Not all the time—things haven't gotten that out of hand, but sometimes it does happen. The only time I smiled during my marathon training was when I got to the end of an organized race and they were handing out a ridiculous amount of free food. Free food always makes me happy. Especially when its presence marks the end of my physical activity for the day.

I think I've narrowed down the possible reasons why biking doesn't incite the homicidal urges usually brought on when I engage in exercise:

1) I can actually ride and talk at the same time. And not just my normal cussing to myself—I can ride with other people and actually carry on a conversation. Like, with full sentences and stuff. This is extremely helpful in passing the time and tends to get my mind off the fact that I'm exerting effort. It is amazing what my body is capable of doing if my mind isn't constantly chiming in with its two cents, *Uh, we're moving. This is not good. I don't like this. Let's stop this. If you don't stop this, I'm going to start singing a Backstreet Boys song over and over and over. Just the chorus, 'cause I don't know the rest. Don't push me.* And then come the homicidal urges.

>>>

>>>

I know that the reason I'm able to talk is that I'm able to breathe. And the reason I'm able to breathe is probably that I'm not really pushing myself too hard. Which probably means that I'm once again going to find myself at the end of most races in which I compete. But I've long since given up the hope of actually being a stellar athlete. Is it so wrong that I like to incorporate a little relaxation into my endurance sports? Which leads to . . .

2) This sport involves coasting. I know it sounds silly, but I'm pretty sure that 90 percent of my smiling occurs when I'm coasting. How much do I love that I can actually stop pedaling but keep moving? It's awesome. In any other sport, your only option for a little rest is to stop what you are doing and sit down for a breather. With cycling I can stop moving my body while my bike keeps chugging along. What a champ.

If I get a little tired or my butt feels like it really could be in need of medical attention, I can just stop pedaling for a few seconds or stand up and let my poor bum relax for a min-ute. I love coasting so much that sometimes I do it until the very last second possible before falling off the bike. I've had people ride by me and ask if I was okay because I was moving so slowly. I'd be smiling ear to ear. "I'm great!" I really like to maximize a coast.

And the hills; oh, the hills. Sure, getting up them is not fun at all, but coasting down them makes the world take on a little brighter tone. You know, it reminds me of how people describe what it feels like to have their first child, the hope and wonder and light that it brings into their life. I can now relate to those people. Not because I have a kid, but because

>>>

>>>

I've coasted down a hill after a hard climb. I know it's wrong to compare this feeling to having a newborn child. 'Cause newborns puke and cry, and going down a hill doesn't have any negative attributes. It is pure joy. On the other hand, going *up* a hill—*that* can involve a lot of puking and crying.

CHAPTER three
The Riding

C ycling is a very interesting sport because it can be done for so many different purposes. Up to this point in the book, I've been focused on information geared toward getting you to complete a century ride, and yet I'd say a vast majority of people who consider themselves "cyclists" or "riders" probably haven't actually done a century ride. (This might have something to do with the fact that these people also consider themselves sane and fans of their butt muscles, but I digress.)

Riding is a lot of different things to a lot of different people. To some, it's a way to get around town or to avoid rush-hour traffic. To some, it's a way to be part of a community, a social outlet with a little bit of exercise thrown in for good measure. For others, it is the best and only way to see various foreign countries, a different way to travel. Then there are those who simply like to hop on their bikes with a group of like-minded individuals and visit the many bars that their fine city has to offer.

Cyclists have a lot of range, is my point.

In the following pages, I'll delve into the different things you can do now that you've got that shiny new bike of yours. It's not all about butt balm and spandex—you can have a lot of fun with cycling, too. So read on and let me introduce you to all the good times that come when you tackle life on two wheels.

Ride to Race

If you are new to cycling and are hoping that you will fall in love with it and immediately become a fit and trim cycling god(dess), you may become a little frustrated with yourself when you lose interest in your divinity after a mere two weeks of riding. Sometimes things that are started with excitement and fervor (and often a large helping of delusion) can fade away through nothing more dramatic than life (*Fresh Prince of Bel-Air* reruns) just getting in the way. If you find yourself in this position and the sheer force of your willpower and focus doesn't prove quite enough to keep you riding, it may help you to begin training for a specific event. Something about putting an event on your calendar and paying the registration fee can be the extra nudge you need when you are debating between ordering pizza and going out for a thirty-minute ride. (Make it a twenty-eight-minute ride, and you can get back in time to meet the thirty-minutes-or-less pizza guy. I'm just sayin', there's no reason you can't have it all.)

Charity rides are one way to go, but if you don't want to deal with the fundraising aspect of a charity ride, there are plenty of fundraising-free rides available for you to tackle. These rides range from the light and merry to the long and torturous. I'd say your best bet would be to find a ride somewhere in the middle—one that is going to require some actual training on your part, but not one that is going to require a 911 call on your behalf. It's important to find balance in all things, you know.

As with any sort of training, you are going to have a lot easier time holding yourself responsible for your required riding if there is someone else holding you responsible as well, so do your best to find someone to train for your event with you. It should be an easy sell, especially because you aren't asking that person to do any of the dreaded fundraising that often accompanies such training. All that will really be required is that the person shows up, rides alongside you, and occasionally says, "No, we can't stop for tacos instead of finishing our ride." You might want to enlist a vegetarian friend, just to make sure she isn't tempted by your sure-to-be-compelling pro-taco argument.

Below are examples of some of the different rides out there just waiting for you to conquer them. After you're done, you can eat all the tacos you want.

50 STATES AND 13 COLONIES RIDE

http://waba.org/events/50states.php

This is an example of a fun ride that offers a good distance but also an interesting theme. The 50 States ride travels for sixty miles around the streets of Washington, D.C., which are all named after different states. The ride covers, you guessed it, the streets named after all fifty states. It's an extremely challenging ride, but also a cool way to see D.C.

The 13 Colonies ride is a shorter version of the 50 States ride, covering only about fifteen miles and visiting the streets named after the original thirteen colonies. Both of these rides are with traffic in urban areas. Take this into consideration when deciding on your race of choice: Battling cars in addition to muscle aches, exhaustion, and butt rashes might be just enough to push you over the edge. Good news is, cabs are easy to find in urban areas.

SEATTLE TO PORTLAND BICYCLE CLASSIC

http://cascade.org/EandR/stp

This is a huge event in the Pacific Northwest that hosts up to ten thousand bikers for a two-hundred-mile ride over one or two days. (I'd say you'd want to aim for two days, 'cause you'd also probably want to aim for not perishing.) The route from Seattle to Portland offers a beautiful ride and an insanely impressive story to tell your friends. And let's be honest: The beautiful ride fades away over time, while the "One time I rode my bike from Seattle to Portland—yeah, I know I'm awesome" one lasts forever.

CINDERELLA CLASSIC

http://valleyspokesmen.org/cinderella_classic.php

This is an all-women, sixty-five- or ninety-five-mile event in California at which people decorate their helmets in various Cinderella-type themes. In my opinion, anytime decorations and/ or themes get involved, things can only turn out well.

Races like this are fun because they add a little creativity to the mix and give you a chance to smile throughout the race. Anything that is working toward getting you to smile while you are riding a bike for hours at a time is always a good addition to an event. Also, if you are a woman, sometimes women-only events can prove to be more laid-back and have a sisterly feel to them. Expect lots of hugs. And maybe even a little happy crying. It happens.

ROSARITO ENSENADA

http://rosaritoensenada.com

I'm including this ride because I've heard from several cyclists that it is a great time. Unfortunately, the event seems to be on hold right now. It doesn't look to be completely dead, so I'm hoping that it will live to ride again.

The event itself is a fifty-mile ride in Mexico, from Rosarito to Ensenada, ending with a great party that lasts long into the night. This is an example of a ride that you'd pick as much for its location as for the race itself. You get a fun ride out of it, and then you can stay for a few extra days and enjoy the beach. Again, I'm hoping this makes a comeback. Once I hear about an event involving chips and salsa and margaritas, it's very hard for me to let it go. If it weren't for all that pesky riding you have to do beforehand, this event would be perfect.

DEATH RIDE

http://deathride.com

Um. This race has the word *death* in it, for God's sake. I'm putting it on this list to show you the extremes you can go to if you so choose. If I were you, I'd so choose to start out with a chips-and-salsa ride first, then work my way up to Death from there. But that's just me, and I'm a sucker for salsa.

This ride is 129 miles and includes fifteen thousand wonderful feet of climbing (methinks that's where the "death" label comes into play). If you aren't feeling like doing the entire ride, there are options to do shorter routes that are perhaps just "serious" and "critical," instead of all the way dead.

This is a very small sampling of the numerous cycling events out there. I've listed them just to give you a rough idea of the kinds of rides available to you. If you want to get a full grasp of the countless cycling events available, you can visit sites like www.bikeride.com or www.active.com to find and register for many a cycling event. Active.com is an especially good site because you can simply put in your location and a date range for your would-be event, and voilà, like magic (and a little like a database, too), it'll give you a list of races to choose from. Find one that looks fun and challenging (and has a cute commemorative race shirt) and register away!

Checklist:
What I'm Looking for in a Race

I've devised a handy little checklist to help you find a race for yourself from among the roughly two kazillion possibilities out there. This list should narrow the options down to only a few thousand. After that, you are going to need to employ the time-tested "Close Your Eyes and Stick Out Your Finger, Then Sign Up for the First Race You Touch" selection tool. I know people who've named their children that way, so it should also serve you well in your race selection efforts. Of course, little Slyvan Monroe might not totally agree.

❏ FLEXIBLE MILEAGE

I want an event that offers me a challenging ride, if I am inclined to take on that challenge, but also several other distances, in case the word "challenging" seems to apply to a shorter distance on race day.

>>>

❏ HILLS

Bring on the burn!

❏ A FLAT RIDE

Burning is overrated, I've found.

❏ POSSIBLE DEATH

I'm looking to challenge myself beyond what seems altogether healthy or intelligent. I need big mileage, big hills, and lots of medication.

❏ A GOOD POSTEVENT PARTY

More than testing the physical limits of silly things like muscles and willpower, I would like to test the limits of my arms to balance as much free food and beverages in them as humanly possible. I am a warrior; I will not be surpassed.

❏ A GREAT LOCATION

I'm all for no pain, no gain, but I feel as though there would be even more gain if, after I completed my race, I were in a desirable location. Preferably one with a bar and/or a beach nearby.

❏ I AM COMFORTABLE WITH CITY RIDING

Bring on the motorists! I have no problem spending my entire race on busy streets full of cars. In fact, if I practice, I might be able to hold on to the back of some of their bumpers for at least a few miles at a time.

❏ I WANT A PRETTY RIDE

If I'm going to torture my body, at least let me have a nice view. I need mountains! I need rolling countryside! I need natural wonder! And I am probably going to need a deep-tissue massage, too, just FYI.

>>>

❏ A LARGE NUMBER OF PARTICIPANTS

I like to ride with the masses, to feel a part of something greater than me, to be led along with the excitement of a huge group of athletes. (And also, the more people, the greater the chance that the postride party will rock. See above.)

❏ A SMALL NUMBER OF PARTICIPANTS

I don't need to be with a big group. I'd prefer to ride with a more manageable number of people. This will increase my odds of being well tended to if/when I collapse halfway up the first big hill.

❏ A FUN THEME

Maybe there are costumes involved, or perhaps live music and the occasional midrace dance break. Whatever it is, I'm looking for an event that offers me a little more entertainment than just the prerace ritual of watching all the cyclists applying Butt Butter.

❏ _____

(Date Range for My Event)

❏ _____

(Other)

❏ _____

(Other)

Ride to Work

A bike is, more than anything, an alternative form of transportation. It is a way to get from point A to point B using something other than an automobile. Unlike other forms of exercise, biking can serve a function beyond simply burning calories and testing your athletic endurance. Technically, I'm sure you could start running everywhere after you take up marathon training, but you might have to start allowing a lot more time for travel. ("I'm heading out now, Jim. I'll meet you at your house next Tuesday. Yay, running!")

Commuting to work is a great way to get in some cycling time, and it's generally just a cool thing to do. Whether you are training for a race or are just cycling for the health benefits, commuting to work can be a nice addition to your biking adventures. As gas prices rise and the environment continues to suffer, more and more people are choosing their bikes over their cars, so not only will you be having fun on your bike, but you will be extremely hip at the same time.

Giving up your car for your commute is a big deal, so make sure you've got a good plan of attack before you blindly leave one morning on your bike in hopes of making it to work in time for an important meeting. This might end with your ditching your bike after four blocks and hitchhiking the rest of the way. And that could end in several bad ways. Below I've listed some tips to get you started on your road to being an environmentally hip urban bike commuter. Look at you!

Look for Friends at Work

If you are unsure about venturing into a new activity, whatever that activity may be, it's always easier to take it on if you can learn from people who already know what they are doing. The best part of this is that you are getting advice from people who have already worked out all their "oh, that really didn't work at all" issues and can save you from having to learn those lessons through your own failures.

The first thing you should do if you are thinking about riding your bike to work is see if you can find someone who is already riding their bike to your place of work. This person will be a great source of information and might even be someone you could ride to work with occasionally. Ask around the office and see if you can find anyone who rides to work or even knows someone in your building or area who does. Then promptly begin stalking this person for everything they know about bicycle commuting.

If you can't find a fellow bicycle commuter via the standard word-of-mouth route, you might try hanging out in the area of your office building that's designated for cyclists to lock up their bikes. That area would be a great place to meet people who are riding their bike to work (or perhaps people who are trying to steal the bikes of people who are riding their bike to work). Either way, you are sure to get a good conversation going. Don't be shy about talking to some random people unlocking their bikes in your office building. Cyclists are generally pretty cool people, and I'm willing to go out on a limb here in asserting that nine times out of ten, the person you approach is going to be happy to share some info with you. Maybe you can offer to buy her lunch one day so you can pick her brain. If she doesn't take you for a complete nut job, it'll be worth your time.

Join a Bike Club

If you are unable to find someone at work to absorb information from, most major cities have at least a few bike clubs that meet and do rides around different areas of town. There aren't usually any formal meeting or membership requirements, but if you are thinking about becoming a bicycle commuter, it would serve you well to get to know other cyclists so you can take advantage of all of their hard-earned knowledge about the sport and commuting. You might even find a person or two to commute with, making your travels even more enjoyable (especially if they just let you follow them around and aren't bothered when you ask them to change your tires when they go flat).

Map Your Route

Take a weekend day or two to map out the best route for your biking commute, first by computer, then by car, then by bike. You can use MapQuest.com to look up various highway-free routes to work, then hop in your car and see where those routes actually take you. You want to try to avoid really busy streets and overly hilly treks. When you're riding a bike to work, the shortest route (in time and in distance) is not always the best route. The goal is to arrive at work and return home in one piece and not completely miserable from the effort. It will be worth your while to find the route that is easiest on you physically and is also the safest, so that your commute goes well. If there is any way for you to incorporate a bike path into any part of your commute, take that option. There is no need to spend any more time with motorists than is absolutely necessary.

Once you've come up with a route you think is good, do a few test runs on a day that doesn't require you to actually get to your place of employment at a specific time. This will relieve a little of the stress of your new adventure, and will give you the chance to work out some kinks (i.e., figure out how to drink your Starbucks coffee while pedaling down Main Street).

Take a Bike Maintenance Class

For me, one of the scariest things about riding around surface streets and off bike paths is that when something goes wrong, I can't very well just sit there looking pathetic until the next knowledgeable cyclist rides by to save me. And other than my ability to look pathetic, I have very few skills that are helpful in fixing bike problems.

If you have repair skills like mine, and you encounter a maintenance problem with your bike while you are trying to get to work, you are going to find yourself in a slight predicament. And a slight predicament can lead to a major panic attack if you find yourself stranded on the side of the road thirty minutes before you're supposed to be in a meeting. One way to help prevent this type of panic attack, and to manage your general unease about counting on your bike, is to actually educate yourself on the bike. I know, it's a revolutionary thought.

Many bike stores offer general bike maintenance classes once or twice a week for little or no cost. You can also find bicycle experts who advertise via little flyers at cycle shops. You can pay them to teach you the wonders of bicycle maintenance in a few one-on-one sessions. In addition to these options, you can usually find much more in-depth classes at your local community college. This might seem like overkill, but think of all the interesting conversations you can start at parties with your knowledge of cogs and lubes (be careful with that combination, though, as it might lead to a totally different conversation).

Learn How to Fix a Flat

You are most likely going to get some flat tires over the course of your commuting. The thought of this may be a bit frightening at first, but eventually it will become old hat to pull over, change or patch your flat, and be on your way.

You should practice changing a tire a few times at home so that your first few tries aren't while you're out on your ride to work. You don't have to do the entire change, but it would be worth it to at least take the tire off the bike, remove the tire from the rim, and then put the whole thing back together. Otherwise you will be like me, having to rely on others to change your numerous flat tires. It's not something I'm proud of, I assure you.

One way to help avoid getting flat tires in the first place is to get tougher, heavier tires. They will weigh you down a bit, but not in any way that you will notice during commuting. And the peace of mind you will get from having tougher tires will be more than worth a slight loss of speed.

How to Change a Flat

If you are doing any significant amount of riding, you are going to get a flat tire at some point during your riding adventures. In fact, sometimes the flat tires are what lead to the adventures, so they aren't all bad. What *can* be all bad is if you have no idea how to change a flat and you are nowhere near anyone who will take pity on your pathetic state and stop to help you.

Below I will outline how to change a tire, but the best way to learn is by doing. And you might want to try out the doing before your first midride flat. That way, you will be prepared and not completely traumatized by the experience. Also, watching someone actually do the various tire-changing steps might make the process a little easier to grasp. If you're a learn-by-watching type of person, ask one of your cycling buddies, or your local Bike Maintenance Dude, to demonstrate for you. (They might be suspicious if you don't ask until your tire is already flat). As an alternative, you can peruse the Internet for helpful videos detailing how to change a tire.

The following are two recognized ways to change your flat tire:

DAWN'S TWO-STEP FLAT TIRE-CHANGING METHOD

Step 1. Look pathetic.

Step 2. Wait for someone to notice your patheticness and offer to change your tire for you.

REST OF THE WORLD'S TIRE-CHANGING METHOD

1. Remove the tire from the bike. If you are removing the front tire, simply open your brakes using the little lever on the side of your brakes. Then move down to the

>>>

center of your tire, where you will find another lever—the quick-release lever. Pull that quick-release lever down and loosen the bolt on the other side of the tire. This will loosen the tire, making it easy to pull off the bike. If you are removing your rear tire, you first need to shift all the way down so that your chain is on your smallest cog and smallest chainwheel, making your chain loose and easier to maneuver a tire around. Open your rear brakes using the brake lever, and open and loosen the quick-release in the center of the tire. Next, pull the tire off by lifting it gently off the bike and away from the chain. Sometimes you will need to lightly guide the chain off the tire with your hand as well.

2. Once the tire is off, spin it around in your hands, examining it and trying to find the source of your flat. If the source of the puncture is still in the tire, remove it and make a note of its location on the tire. Making note of the puncture location is a critical step if you want to patch the tube once it's out of the tire. Otherwise, you will be spending a lot of time randomly searching for what may be a hard-to-find hole.

3. Fully flatten the tire either by unscrewing the top of the valve and pressing down (presta valve), or by sticking something sharp into the valve of your shrader valve. If you have a presta valve, you are going to need to unscrew it from the base of the tire as well, so that it can be removed.

4. Get two tire levers and a fresh tube out of your saddlebag. Wedge one tire lever between the tire and the rim of the tire, then pull the lever down. This should pop the tire edge out from the rim. Once you've done this, hook the other end of the tire lever to the closest rim to hold it in place.

>>>

5. Next, wedge in a second tire lever, but this time you are going to slowly move the lever around the diameter of the rim, forcing the tire away from the rim as you go. Eventually, you'll make your way back to your first tire lever, and one entire side of your tire should be free from the rim.

6. Pull the tire and tube completely off the rim.

7. Run your fingers gently over the rim of the tire, checking to see if there are any foreign, tire-popping objects in or along the rim. It would be a shame to replace the whole tire, only for it to be popped again by something you didn't remove.

8. Remove your punctured tube from the tire.

9. Run your hands along the inside of the tire, checking for foreign, tire-popping objects here as well. Also take note of any gaping holes in your tire itself. If there is a hole, then your new tube is going to be vulnerable in that spot and pop all over again. Do your best to patch any tire holes before getting back on the bike. These patches are temporary at best, and you should go get a new tire as soon as you can.

10. If you have the kit and the inclination, you can patch your punctured tube using a patch kit. If you aren't feeling patchy, then grab your new tube and fill it slightly with air, just enough to give it shape.

11. Put the new or patched tube back into the tire.

12. Put the tire back around the tire rim.

13. Put the tire on the ground and slowly work one side of the tire back into the rim using your palms and your

>>>

thumbs. Make sure that none of the tube is sticking out between the tire and the rim.

14. Turn the tire over and push the other side of the tire into the rim. If it is too tight a fit, you can use your levers to help wedge the tire back in.

15. Check the diameter of the tire on both sides, making sure that the tube is not sticking out anywhere.

16. Reinflate the tube with a hand pump or CO_2 cartridge.

17. Put the tire back on the bike, making sure to close the brake and quick-release levers you opened when removing the tires. Trying to ride without brakes (or tires) is a great way to destroy all the pride you built up from your tire-changing skills.

Take Care of Your Bike

The best way to handle maintenance problems on your commute is to not have maintenance problems on your commute. And the best way to ensure that is to take good care of your bike. See "Taking Care of Your Bike" in Chapter 1 for more details and helpful tips. Every weekend, you should give your bike a once-over to make sure everything is looking good. Check your tire pressure and make sure there isn't any noticeable wear and tear on the brakes, chains, or tires. Once a month or so, you might also clean your bike and make it shiny and new again. The wear and tear from spending every day on roads and from the elements can cause a lot of grime and buildup.

It's a good idea to take your bike in for regular maintenance at the bike shop, just to have a professional look it over and see if there is anything that needs to be fixed. This could probably be an every-few-months thing until you get really comfortable with your bike's mechanics and maintenance.

Commuting Accessories

Commuting to work successfully is going to involve buying even more accessories for your bike. I know, just when you thought your credit card was safe, I present you with even more things to dent it. However, most of these items are going to add to your overall enjoyment and happiness while commuting to and from work. Enjoyment and happiness on your commute will translate into happier times at work and when you get home from work, so spring for these items if you need them. Your coworkers and family will thank you for it.

PANIER BAGS

These are made for touring cyclists, people who wish to travel the world on the back of a bike and therefore need to carry all of their necessities with them. You aren't touring the world, but you are embarking on a tour of sorts every day, in that you will be ending up in a different place than where you started your trip. This means that you will need to bring some things along with you.

There are many panier bags designed specifically for commuters, so you don't have to walk around carrying an awkward pack at work. Some of the cooler designs feature a knapsack that clips onto and off your rack on the back of your bike, so it's easy to transport and easy to walk around with during the day.

FENDERS

Fenders fit over your front and/or back tire and can be very effective at keeping you dry and clean. City streets can be less than immaculate, and bike tires have a way of picking up all that messiness and throwing it at your legs and body. This tendency is even worse when you are driving in wet, rainy conditions. If you don't want to arrive at work looking like you just stepped out of a mud puddle, fenders are a good investment.

CHAINGUARDS

Chainguards come in some styles that cover part of your chain and others that cover the entire chainwheel. These are good buys because they will help keep your chain clean, as well as help keep your pant leg from coming into contact with the dirty chain throughout your ride.

LIGHTS/REFLECTORS

Lights and reflectors are imperative for commuters. You will be riding amid many cars, and it's important that you are seen before you are sprawled out on the hood of one of them. Always err on the side of abundance when putting lights on your bike. Sure, you may look like some sort of year-round Christmas celebration, but at least you'll be noticed (and probably made fun of as well—but chuckles at your expense don't hurt as bad as bumpers on your legs).

LOCK

You're going to need a good lock if you plan to leave your bike unattended outside all day. Depending on the location of your office and the security available for your bike, you may want to invest in a heavy-duty U lock that is nearly robber-proof. It is also as heavy as said robber, so it will weigh you down quite a bit, which is something you'll want to take into consideration.

Some riders also take the added precaution of locking their seat to the bike so that they don't return to a lovely bike with no sitting option available.

HEADPHONES

I'm listing headphones, but I actually recommend that you don't use them. If you insist on using headphones, please use only one earpiece, leaving the other ear open to hear all of the wonders of rush hour. (The unique combination of tire screeches, cuss words, and drive-time DJs is almost a symphony in itself—who needs MP3s?)

Packing

The biggest headache involved in commuting to work is what to do about your work clothes. I have friends who ride to work in their work clothes every day, then hop off their bike and walk into their office without looking like they just completed an outdoor racing event. One friend who does says the secret is not wearing a backpack of any sort on your commute. This will keep your back from sweating and prevent the ensuing stinkiness.

A lot of commuters don't feel comfortable riding in their work attire, so they come up with alternate ways of getting their stuff to work. One commuter I talked to said she works with her wife, whose car acts as a huge panier bag. If you aren't lucky enough to have a spouse who is willing to transport all of your work necessities for you, you'll need to decide how and when you're going to get those necessities to your office.

One option is to keep a small supply closet (or drawer) at work with any whatnots you may need. You can keep a couple pairs of shoes, a towel, some deodorant, some shampoo (in case of a mandatory shower), perfume or cologne, and a toothbrush and toothpaste. As far as your daily clothes go, you can either carry them with you or simply bring the entire week's wardrobe with you on Monday. That sounds like a lot of forethought for a Monday, but preferences undoubtedly vary. No matter what, always keep an extra change of clothes and accessories at the office, just in case you get to work and realize you forgot something sort of important, like a shirt. I imagine that even on casual Fridays, wearing a jersey around the office might be difficult to play off.

Be Safe

You don't want to waste your precious sick days on commuting-related accidents, so do your best to be safe out there on the roads. With some basic considerations in mind, you should be able to arrive safely at your destination every day and be able to save up your PTO for a worthwhile cause, like a hangover.

The number one rule of bike safety is to be visible to motorists. The reality is that drivers aren't actually looking to run you over, even though you may feel like they are. Help them in their efforts to avoid hitting you by being as visible as possible. Wear reflectors and lights so they can see you before they get to you.

Also, do your best to stay off of sidewalks. They may seem like a safer place to ride, but drivers probably won't notice you up there, and you may have a problem when you surprise a motorist as you leave a sidewalk and unexpectedly enter an intersection.

Remember that at certain times of the day, the sun will be at just the right spot in the sky to make it very difficult for drivers to see anything out of their front windows, including you and all of your various visibility aids. You might want to try to avoid riding at these times, or at the very least be extra cautious with any turns or merges, making sure you make eye contact with drivers before you bike in front of them.

If your commute involves riding on busy city streets, moving cars are not going to be your only obstacles. You should also be very aware of parked cars on the side of the street. Look into the side-view mirrors of these cars to see if anyone is about to make an exit and leave you smashed into a car door. Also be aware of pedestrians emerging from between two parked cars, looking to jaywalk across the street and possibly putting themselves at risk of getting to know your handlebars quite well.

Remember that as a cyclist, you have just as much of a right to be on the road as cars do, but that doesn't necessarily mean that you have the right to take over the road. Drivers are used to dealing with large pieces of machinery that move fast but are pretty predictable on the whole. Cyclists, on the other hand, can move all over the road, weaving in and out of cars, making turns and stops whenever they feel like it. Try not to be one of those cyclists when you're riding with traffic. Try to ride your bike the same way you would drive your car. Be predictable in your actions, and drivers will be predictable in their reactions to you. I tell you this mostly as a driver who has nearly hit approximately 345,234 cyclists who just sorta decided they'd make up the rules with the hope that I'd react accordingly.

Start Out Small

Not everyone lives close enough to work for bike commuting to be a feasible option. If you're one of these people, you might consider combining your bike with some public transportation. It's a good and cheap way to get around your city, and it could make your dreams of bike commuting a reality.

A good tip for those of you considering any kind of bike commuting: Start out small. Maybe start by cycling to work on Mondays or Fridays and work your way up to more days. If you want to make bike commuting a long-term activity, make sure you don't burn out on it and go fleeing back to your car after two weeks. Also, make sure you still have the ability to drive to work if you need to. Don't give up your parking spot at work, or at least make sure you have a backup location that you can use if you need to drive in one day. Nothing will make you long for your car commute more than thinking about the fact that you can no longer drive when you need or want to.

Ride Around Town

Beyond commuting, more and more people are embracing cycling as a general means of transportation to places other than work. This is obviously not an option if you live fifty miles away from everything you need to get to, but cycling is an excellent way to bop around to nearby places.

City planners and officials in many of the more populated cities throughout the United States are slowly coming to realize that they have quite a few people traveling in quite a few cars within their city limits. As this becomes clear, they are also realizing that if they can get some of those people out of their cars and onto bikes, negative things like traffic and pollution can be reduced. If you take a minute next time you're in a big city, you might notice the bike-friendly systems that are in place, with more bike lanes and better parking options for those who travel on two wheels.

Riding a bike to professional sports events or concerts can save you a lot of time and money because you don't have to pay for parking or spend a half hour after the event trying to remember if you parked in section A or Q. Plus, bicycle parking is always right up front and some places even offer bike valet service: You stand there and wait for the valet, along with the other customers, and the dude pulls up on your bike. Never mind showing up the SUV owners; you'll totally outdo the environmentally conscious Prius owners, too. What could be more fun?

Ride for a Cause

Charity is one of the most significant reasons people randomly decide to take up cycling. Which is ironic, since I always feel like I am in need of some sort of charity right after I get *off* my bike. (Make donations to "Dawn's Saddle Sores: End the Agony in Our Lifetime" today.) Charity rides of all sizes are constantly popping up around the country and abroad, making it easier than ever to ride for a cause greater than yourself (and fantastic leg muscles).

Am I the only one who finds it a bit disconcerting that physical exhaustion and the overall pain of your fellow man are fast becoming the biggest inspirations for charitable giving? "Bob, I was wondering if you'd like to donate to the Cure the World of Everything Foundation. It's tax deductible." "Um, no, I don't really have any extra cash right now." "What if I risk my life and my sanity by training for a ridiculous endurance event that will probably make me cry?" "Hmmm, in that case, put me down for $50." It's a bit troubling, is all I'm saying. But it's also raising an assload of money for some great causes, so I guess a little masochism isn't always a bad thing.

If you are the kind of person who gets super excited about starting a new sport, only to become super excited about your couch about two weeks later, then training for a charity event might be a good fit for you. Believe you me, I am an expert in all things couch, from its offering of endless horizontal time to its usually close proximity to a television of some sort. And don't get me started on pillows. I understand your plight. And I understand how much more alluring your couch looks when compared with the option of sitting on a hard bicycle seat for hours on end (namely on your end).

The good thing about doing a charity ride is that it increases your odds of actually choosing the bike over the couch. And anything that increases the odds of your actually cycling should be a welcome addition to your cycling training plan. When you decide to do a race for charity, you're suddenly presented with two stark options: "Sit on the coach and eat Funyuns" or "Ride my bike and raise money for a good cause." Depending on your overall mood and hunger level, more times than not the good cause is going to beat out the Funyuns. If chocolate comes into play, all bets are off.

The best part about doing a charity ride is that with every donation you accept, you are in essence making a promise to the donor that you will actually be participating in said charity ride. If you are like me (and I do feel a special bond with you) and the promises you make to other people are much more difficult to break than promises you make to yourself, then a charity ride is definitely the way to go. Without that commitment, you might be just as happy with the promise of chocolate and Funyuns as with the promise of a ten-mile bicycle ride. Thing is, training for a cause greater than yourself is a big deal, and blowing off your training makes you kind of a jerk. In addition to the guilt you'll feel from being a lazy ass, you will also feel the guilt of letting down an entire charitable organization and the people it supports. Which is great! Look, if general enthusiasm and actual desire can't be your motivation to cycle, there is no reason why good old-fashioned guilt can't substitute. Any decent mother should have taught you this little life lesson long ago.

The Rides

If you are thinking about training for a cause, there are plenty of causes looking for you, so it's really a matter of picking one whose overall good work and lifesaving mission seem like a fair trade-off for your being made to wear padded spandex shorts in public. It's important that you pick a charity that you care about, at least a little bit, because it really will help you stay motivated as the weeks wear on. You don't want to be the one yelling out: "Honestly, I couldn't give a crap if the elementary school gets a new flagpole—I'm done with this!" Also, it will be much easier for you to raise money for a charity whose work you are a fan of than to find yourself unsure of the reason you're out there: "I don't know, it's patriotic or something—look, just give me five bucks. I'm wearing a butt pad, for God's sake."

There are a crazy number of charity rides out there, so there is no way I can list them all. But I guess I can *begin* to list them all. I'll begin below, in no particular order:

AIDS LIFECYCLE

www.aidslifecycle.org

This is a very popular and very well-known charity ride in support of the San Francisco AIDS Foundation and the L.A. Gay & Lesbian Center. It travels 545 miles from San Francisco to Los Angeles over the course of seven days. Cyclists raise $3,000 each and participate in an amazing journey with thousands of other riders and fun support staff.

I know several people who have done this event, some more than once, and all of them have nothing but positive things to say about it. When you consider the fact that they spent seven days riding their bikes and sleeping in tents, it says a lot about the event that every single one of them uses the word "amazing" when describing the experience. If you look a little further into this ride, though, you'll find out why "amazing" is used so freely. This ride has something no other ride has: drag queens. There are drag queens at the pit stops and drag queens cheering on riders along the route. And I don't know about you, but I feel like anytime drag queens are around, good times are mandatory.

This ride fills up fast, so if you are interested, register early. They don't make any exceptions for anyone who forgets to register. Even if you happen to be writing a book about cycling and would love to make the race a part of it. So I've heard. Ahem.

BIG RIDE ACROSS AMERICA

http://cleanairadventures.org/big_ride_across_america

The title of this forty-eight-day ride sorta says it all. It's a *big* ride. Across America.

Cyclists raise $6,000 each for the American Lung Association of the Northwest, and for that donation they get to ride their happy butts 3,300 miles from Seattle to Washington, D.C. 'Cause, you know, that doesn't sound crazy *at all*. The event website says it's "life simplified to ride, eat, and sleep," which actually doesn't sound all that *simple* to me. It's the *riding* part that's got me a little worried; the eat-and-sleep part, I feel ready for.

If you are looking for a big event and a way to see this great country of ours, this might be just what you've been waiting for. I myself am going to keep waiting for the event that is just "life simplified to sleep."

MS BIKE RIDES

www.bikems.org

MS Bike Rides holds around one hundred events throughout the year, all over the country. The events raise money for multiple sclerosis (MS), and many are two-day, 150-mile rides. The website listed above has links to the various events throughout the land. Maybe you can hit some them as you ride through town with the Big Ride Across America. You'd be funding cures left and right.

TEAM IN TRAINING CENTURY RIDE

www.teamintraining.org/firsttimehere/sportprograms/centuryridescycle

Team in Training is best known for its marathon training programs, but it is expanding into century rides as well. Participants receive personalized training schedules and support in exchange for raising funds for the Leukemia & Lymphoma Society.

Team in Training does not put on actual events; it merely trains cyclists to participate in century rides that are put on by other organizations. Cycling with Team in Training is a fun way to experience an event because it allows you to feel like you are part of a group in what can often be a very intimidating mass of people. Most events are well staffed and can accommodate any needs you may have along the route, but going to an event with a group like Team in Training gives you the security of knowing that there are coaches and volunteers there specifically for you. Maybe for a couple other people on your team, too, but mostly just for you.

This organization has had quite a bit of success in the marathon training world, which means that most people have heard of it. This name recognition is very helpful when you are asking people to make donations. Not that your friends would be suspicious of you otherwise—"The charity is called Children in Need of Daily Insulin? Cindi, I gotta be honest, that sounds a little shady."

BIKE AND BUILD
http://bikeandbuild.org

This organization supports affordable housing and caters mainly to younger people in search of a productive way to spend their summer vacation. For those college students looking to do more than perfect their beer pong technique during their break, Bike and Build gives them the chance to travel, exercise, and do a little good along the way. Don't worry, you have the rest of your life to worry about beer pong.

Young cyclists raise $4,000 and spend a couple summer months making their way across different parts of the grand old USA. Along the way, they have scheduled "Build Days," when the group takes a day off from cycling to work on an affordable-housing project in an area it's visiting. Although this ride sounds a little bit like a program for wayward youth, it also sounds like a really cool way to spend some time before heading back to school.

GET YOUR GUTS IN GEAR
www.ibdride.org

Can we please just take a moment to note the name of this organization? Please? Oh, wait . . . first take note of the fact that these rides are raising money for the Crohn's & Colitis Foundation of America. As in digestive diseases. Get Your Guts in Gear? Really?

If you are able to get past the name of these rides, they seem like they might be a good time (a much better time than digestive diseases, I'll tell you that much). There are three, three-day rides (in Texas, New York, and Washington state) benefiting digestive systems the nation over. Each ride is 210 miles total and, I have to assume, involves a T-shirt that actually says GET YOUR GUTS IN GEAR. Which to me is reason enough to do the event.

PAN-MASSACHUSETTS CHALLENGE
www.pmc.org

This event is held in Massachusetts and offers quite a variety of riding options. With over 4,000 cyclists, the event is the biggest endurance-sports fundraiser in the country. Participants raise money for cancer research and can choose between several one- or two-day rides for up to 192 miles of cycling. The routes vary in difficulty, which provides a nice alternative to those who might want to participate but don't want to pass away.

BEST BUDDIES CHALLENGE
http://bestbuddieschallenge.org

These rides support the Best Buddies organization, which pairs volunteers and people with intellectual disabilities. Cyclists raise at least $1,500 and can choose between one-hundred-, sixty-two-, thirty-five-, and fifteen-mile bike rides. The event hosts a big party at the end, which you can get to much faster if you turn off the hundred-mile route and just do the fifteen-mile trek instead. I'm just sayin'.

The rides I've listed are some of the bigger rides around the country, but there are countless other local rides for good causes. Many of them do not require a large fundraising minimum, which might be a nice relief if some of the numbers listed above are a bit overwhelming. Simply go online and search for "(your city) charity bike ride," and you'll most likely find something to participate in. The only thing to watch out for when searching online are charity motorcycle rides that come up. I imagine you might feel kinda silly showing up in your spandex and helmet to one of those events. But on the upside, I'm sure one of the biker dudes would let you ride on the back of his bike for the entirety of the event.

Charity bike rides can also be found internationally and can offer you the opportunity to combine cycling, travel, and philanthropy (and a little bit of butt soreness, too). If you are considering doing an international event, do a lot of research and make sure to request that information be sent to you detailing the event and the charity it supports. It's not a huge deal if an event near your house turns out to be a bust, but if you travel halfway across the world only to find a ride that is supported by two elderly women and a chicken, you might be a little upset.

Fundraising

When taking on cycling to raise money for charity, many people find the fundraising much more difficult than the training itself (these people are gluttons for punishment, it would seem). It's hard getting money from people, and even more difficult asking for it in the first place. In my opinion, the two keys to fundraising for events like these are repetition and creativity. If you could be creative repeatedly, that would be quite helpful.

REPETITION

Repetition is the key to getting your friends and family to donate to your cause. Overall, people want to support you and your need to inflict harm upon yourself for the sake of bettering the world. But they might need to be reminded of this harm and the bettering on more than one occasion so they can get from the mental-note stage to the actual writing-a-check phase. Send out emails to everyone on a regular basis, reminding them of your training and your cause. Remember to give them plenty of details about both. Some people are going to donate just because you are insane and riding a bike all over the continental United States, while others are going to be drawn to your particular cause. And don't forget to tell people why you were drawn to this particular cause as well. It's important that people know your inspiration so that they too can be inspired. Hopefully their inspiration will turn out better than yours—leading to cash instead of a rash.

CREATIVITY

Creativity is most useful in getting money out of the hands of acquaintances and complete strangers. People have disposable income, and it is your job to trick them into giving it to you. The best way to do that is to grab their attention, and the best way to grab their attention is by implementing a little creativity. Following, I've listed a few examples of successful fundraisers I've heard about or been a part of.

Creative Idea #1

The coolest idea I've heard came from a friend of mine who did the AIDS ride. She and some other friends set up their bikes on trainers outside a couple of businesses. Not trainers as in personal trainers, but the equipment (described on page 86) that turns your regular bike into a stationary bike of sorts, and voilà, you're getting nowhere fast. My friend got nowhere fast outside a local gay bar in town in an effort to raise money for her AIDS ride. She and her fellow riders just pedaled for hours and collected donations from people coming in and out of the bar. (I'm thinking they got more from the people coming out of the bar.)

They also set up their bikes outside REI one weekend and rode all day. They raised a lot of money in both locations because the idea was creative, and because they knew their audience. I doubt this idea would have worked as well if they'd set up outside a minimart. Setting up outside the gay bar meant that they were going to be raising money for a cause that many of the patrons probably felt strongly about. Setting up outside an REI meant that they were going to grab the attention of people who were athletic and might be inclined to support the cause of other movers. This is definitely one of the less complicated fundraising ideas I've ever heard of, and one of the most lucrative ones as well.

Creative Idea #2

Set up a change jar in your office. Encourage the people you work with to throw their spare change in the jar, especially after lunch. This may seem simple, but it can add up over time. I have a friend who raised $250 doing this.

Creative Idea #3

I've heard of karaoke parties where people pay a certain amount to have someone else sing a song. People who don't want to sing have to pay a greater amount to get out of it. It can go back and forth until the person either is made to sing or pays $3,000 to avoid public humiliation. This party works best if you invite only extremely inverted people who would rather mortgage their house than get up in front of people and sing. It probably doesn't work so well if you hang out with people like my friends, who not only love performing but would probably throw in some inappropriate gyrating free of charge.

Creative Idea #4

A friend of mine had a lot of success with a movie night. She projected a movie on a screen outside (you could use a large wall, too) and charged people $10 to get in. She even had popcorn and other snacks for her guests. This sounds like a fun way to get people together for an evening. You could also show a little video about your charity to inspire even more giving. Get people high on caffeine and buttered popcorn, and you never know what will happen.

Creative Idea #5

Have a car wash. Or a dog wash. I know it seems ridiculous, as an adult, to be out there waving signs when there are probably four other car washes going on nearby to benefit the local high school's cheerleading team. But you'd be surprised how many people will pull into a car wash manned by people over the age of fifteen. And you'd be even more surprised how much money they give you. I've considered that it might be out of pity, but don't you worry about that—just have fun with it.

Creative Idea #6

Put on some sort of tournament. Pick a sport that's pretty easy to set up, maybe a soccer, basketball, or softball tournament at a local park. Have everyone pay $20 to play. Put some of that money toward snacks and a couple prizes (cash is fun) and donate the rest to your charity. This is a great way for people to come out and do something fun while getting the chance to support you as well. I might also mention hosting a poker tournament, but gambling is illegal in some places, so pretend I didn't.

Creative Idea #7

Capitalize on the time of year. If it's Christmastime, make something holly and/or jolly for people to buy. If you are not artistically inclined, go to the dollar store and stock up on holly-jolly things and a few coffee mugs. Fill the coffee mugs with holly-jolliness, making them into cute little gifts people will want to buy and give to others when they realize they forgot to buy something for those others. If it's St. Patty's Day, sell something green: cookies, pins, four leaf clovers, whatever. If it's near Mother's Day, sell something cheesy that says something about loving Mom: T-shirts, earrings, flasks, whatever. It's easy, I promise.

If you're wanting to do a fundraising ride, you'll also be wanting to brainstorm seriously about the people you might be able to get money from, and then brainstorm ways in which you might consider doing some fundraising. You can cheat by filling in some of your own answers with things I've already suggested in this chapter. But use this section to mark down your brilliant ideas. You never know—ten years from now, that brilliant money-making scheme you thought up might be all the cycling-fundraising rage.

Fundraising Idea #1

Fundraising Idea #2

Fundraising Idea #3

Fundraising Idea #4

Fundraising Idea #5

Ride the World

People have all sorts of different reasons for jumping into the world of cycling. If you are new to cycling, you most likely took up the sport for health reasons, or perhaps you were looking to challenge yourself by training for a century ride. I fell into the latter category when I decided to buy a bike, strap on my helmet, and ride my happy butt all over the place in the name of training. I was expecting cycling training to be similar to the training I did for a marathon. There wasn't a lot of variety in my marathon-training program; it consisted mainly of running, running, and then some more running thrown in for good measure. I would grudgingly go out five times a week, put in the miles I was supposed to, then return home to take some Advil. I usually ran at one or two possible locations and didn't really get anywhere exciting, besides back to my car (which, at the time, was actually the most exciting thing I could imagine).

When I took on cycling, I took a similar approach to training. I even headed out to the same bike trail where I had done most of my running. The miles were clearly marked and it was a bike-friendly route away from cars, so it seemed like a good fit for the miles I was going to need to get in. But shortly after I started to train, I also started to get a little bit bored with my repeated trips to the same trail to ride the same miles. I started doing more riding on my stationary bike at home, simply because I could at least change my TV station for the variety I was seeking. (Also, watching the sad people on reality shows always makes me feel better about myself—they are a good morale booster that keeps me pedaling along.) While riding an exercise bike is a decent way to work in some miles and build up muscles (mostly the finger muscle, from changing the channel with the remote), it will never be the same as getting outside on your actual bike.

I realized something had to change in my routine, or I'd be in danger of simply losing interest in my training. Because I was immersing myself in all things bike, I decided to explore the world of bike tourism. It seemed like a great way to combine my new sport with my love of random travel. I'm not really into standard touristy stuff, so I'm always looking for interesting ways to see the world. On the back of a bike fit into that category.

My experience traveling through the Swiss Alps on a bike was absolutely amazing. I rode between twenty and fifty miles a day and never once thought about the distance. Well, that's a lie—I thought about it quite a bit when I was struggling up hills, but considerably less when I was riding through an orchard or alongside a rolling meadow. I was shocked to find that I was participating in a sport and not hating every second. It was a big moment for me. And I don't think it was only as a result of the wine we drank at lunch every day.

When I returned home from Switzerland after riding down highways and on winding, two-lane mountainside roads, I was absolutely fearless. No longer did I feel the need to load up my bike and *drive* it to my ride. I now just left straight from my house on my bike, riding a route that I had mapped out beforehand. When I started doing this, I started seeing cycling in a different light. It wasn't just a chore that had to be done; it was a way to get around, a way to see places in ways I never could while riding in a car.

I know that it's not feasible for everyone to incorporate a European cycling adventure into their training schedule (but I'm pretty sure you'd have no problem replicating the cheese-and-wine intake), but that doesn't mean that you can't seek out alternate ways to get your miles in. There is no reason why you need to stay on bike paths or stationary bikes for all of your rides. Go out and explore a little! You've got a helmet and health insurance—you'll be fine.

Adding adventure rides into your training schedule is not only fun, but also a great way to get used to riding with traffic and on different, less than perfect terrains. If you are training for a long-distance event, the odds are that its route is going to wind in and out of different areas, very rarely on streets that have been closed down specifically for your riding convenience. You can't tackle that kind of race without confidence in your ability to both do the miles and do whatever kinds of miles present themselves.

In addition to diversifying your training, exploring the world on a bike is just a really fun thing to do. When I was talking to my Bike Dudes at the local cycle shop, they didn't have much to tell me about training for a century ride. I was confused by this.

"But aren't you guys all supercyclists?"

"Yeah."

"Then how have you not trained for a century ride?"

"We don't really train, we just ride."

With that simple statement, "we just ride," I realized that this thing I had taken on to challenge and possibly traumatize myself was something a lot of people choose to do for a good time. And not in some sort of masochistic way (although I might have to reconsider my assessment of someone's psychological motivations if they confess to actually liking riding up hills).

Below, I've outlined a few ways you can "just ride," too, in your town, your country, your world. Do yourself a favor and do a little exploring with that bike of yours. There is a whole world out there waiting for you to pedal through. On a personal note, I highly recommend stopping for wine and cheese along the way— they tend to make the scenery quite a bit brighter.

Ride in Your City

Maybe you've lived in your city for years, but you miss so much when you zoom around only in your car. Hopping on your bike and riding around your city is not only a fun way to explore your town, but also a great way to save money on gas. A ride around your city can be as simple as taking a bike to the movies instead of the car, or as complicated as planning out an intricate route that gets you from one side of town to the other, with stops along the way for a good lunch or to take in a local sight that you've never quite gotten around to checking out.

If you have kids, riding around town is a great family activity. It'll get them away from the computer, it will wear them out, and it will give you time together. (Just remember, it's simple to avoid any awkward conversation topics that may arise—just pedal faster.) It's also a great way to spend time witha teenagers who might not be all that talkative but who still need to have some memory of your spending time with them between the ages of fourteen and seventeen.

In general, planning out a ride in your own city shouldn't be too difficult. It's likely that you know the area well enough to be able to figure out a suitable route to and from some worthwhile destinations. If you aren't completely sure of a route, map it out in your car first, making sure it's relatively safe for bikes and doesn't involve any crazy hills that you might have ignored when moving yourself with an engine-powered machine.

You can also go to www.mapquest.com and generate a map from your house to wherever you want to go. Just make sure to check the little box that says "Avoid Highways" under the "Routing Options" drop-down menu. This will give you a route that includes only surface streets. The only bad part about using MapQuest is that it's made for drivers of cars, so it obviously doesn't include any possible bike paths that may be available along your route. So there is a possibility you may end up riding farther than you need to because you are staying on streets. If you have a little time to spend, you can most likely find a downloadable online map of any bike trails in your area. If you study that map and the MapQuest map, you will eventually be able to figure out the best route for you. You might want to download the bus route, too, just in case your adventure leaves you longing for motorized transportation.

Another fun thing to do on bikes is an activity called geo-caching. Geocaching is described at www.geocaching.com as "a high-tech treasure hunting game played throughout the world by adventure seekers equipped with GPS devices." I feel like the words "treasure hunting" and "adventure seekers" might be a little bit of an oversell for this activity, but I have a few friends who have done geocaching, and they tell me it's a lot of fun. The basic idea behind it is that there are a bunch of little "treasure" boxes called geocaches (from what I hear, the "treasures" are of the Cracker Jack variety—but 1980s Cracker Jacks, not the lame crap they put in the boxes these days) hidden all over the place.

You start by going to www.geocaching.com and finding out the GPS coordinates where the little boxes are hidden, then use your GPS to map out a route to the boxes. The boxes are hidden in different areas, so your day might entail some walking or hiking, too. Some are hidden in public areas, like in the parking lot of a supermarket, while others are hidden out in the wilderness. You can explore the site to see what your options are and what would be a good fit for you and your group of friends or family.

While people of all ages enjoy geocaching, it sounds like something kids would love, what with the treasure-hunt aspect of it. (I'm not gonna lie—I wouldn't mind hunting down some Cracker Jack prizes myself.) Work with your kids to plot out your hunt route ahead of time, then take off on your bike to find treasure boxes all over your town. Be sure to bring treasures of your own so you can exchange them for any that you take out (they'd better not be lame treasures, either—that's a geocaching faux pas, I've decided).

Ride in the United States

If you've ever had occasion to drive across the country, you know how vast and diverse our landscape is (and exactly how much space is taken up by Middle of Nowhere, USA). Traveling around the United States by bike may seem silly if you feel like you've already seen quite a bit of this country just from your random travels throughout the land.

Bike tourism, however, allows you to take the time to really explore the landscape. There are places to be found that are accessible only by bike, places you would never know existed if a car were the only vehicle you ever traveled around the United States in. It's worth it to take a few days and head out in search of undiscovered territories. It's a fun experience, and also a somewhat humbling reminder of exactly how big this country is.

Riding around the United States can be done with a group or by yourself. Below, I'll outline some of the ways to participate in one of these trips.

WITH OTHERS

There are a lot of group tour options if you are looking to cycle through or around a certain state. Many tour companies that cater to the international market also have bike tourism options within the United States. These can be a fun, stress-free way to see different parts of our country, led by professionals in the bike tourism business.

If you are looking for a slightly cheaper option, search out some of the various tours that bike clubs put on throughout the country. These are usually annual events, rather than regularly occurring trips that you can sign up for at any time.

Riding with a group is always a fun way to travel because of the social opportunities it presents and the pressure it takes off you with regard to lodging and eating arrangements. However, you often end up paying a pretty steep price for these conveniences. If you are up for a little planning and navigating, you could probably save yourself some money by heading out on a ride by yourself.

SELF-GUIDED

Many of the group tours offer their routes as self-guided options to those who might be interested in exploring on their own.

They will assist you with a route sheet and many times set up lodging as well.

If you are up for a true independent adventure, it is possible to ride your bike all the way across the country by yourself. (You might need to save up quite a bit of vacation time first, though, as that Middle of Nowhere, USA, can eat up a lot of time between photo opportunities.)

If you are interested in taking one of these cycling adventures, check out the aptly named Adventure Cycling at www .adventurecycling.org. There you will find a ridiculous collection of maps that wind all around the United States. The routes have been accumulating since 1976 and now cover more than thirty-eight thousand miles of land. They are carefully mapped and tend to lead cyclists through rural and low-traffic roads. These detailed maps can be downloaded or purchased through Adventure Cycling's website.

Around the World

Bicycle tourism is an amazing way to take in the sights that the world has to offer. I really can't say enough good things about it. The world is a very diverse, interesting place, full of nooks and crannies that are waiting to be explored. Bike tours give you a unique opportunity to do more than merely whiz past these nooks and crannies. The routes will invariably run you through open land and into small villages untouched by time. Visiting these places on a bike puts you out in the world, with nothing between you and it. It's hard to explain the feeling, but it would probably be best described as the difference between seeing a pretty rose and stopping to actually smell it. Because you literally can stop to smell the roses when you are traveling via bike. (I also recommend stopping to smell the things that you can eat and drink—because they turn out to hold more long-term satisfaction than smelling roses.)

You have two basic choices once you've decided to do a bike tour. You can choose to go on your own, on what is called a self-guided tour, or you can go out with a group tour. While "self-guided" sounds scary, it is actually quite doable. Many companies offer self-guided versions of their group tours, on which travelers are provided with all the route information and even have hotel and some meal arrangements made for them. If you are someone who enjoys a little adventure and has a good sense of direction, a self-guided tour might be a good fit for you. I'd highly recommend being fluent in the language of the land through which you are guiding yourself, however, because you are more than likely going to require the assistance of a local at some point. A nice translation dictionary or handheld device would be a wise investment if you are heading out onto the random roads of a foreign land alone, I'd say (and I'd say it only in English, 'cause that's the only language I know).

The other, more popular tours are guided group tours that lead a group of people through a particular area. This is the option I recommend, just because it allows you to meet new people and learn about the area you're riding through, and, most important, provides you with at least one person who can speak the native tongue. That native tongue is ever so helpful, if for no other reason than that it can help you figure out exactly what you are ordering off the menu.

There are all sorts of tour companies and types out there for you to choose from. Picking the right tour for you is going to take a little bit of research on your part, but in the long run it will lead you to the best possible trip for you and your two-wheeled friend.

Where

The first decision you need to make is where, exactly, you want to go. Not every place on the planet is best viewed by bicycle, so it's best to pick a place that will give you the most bang for your traveling buck. (Perhaps the Sahara desert might be better toured via Humvee.) What kind of terrain are you looking for? What kinds of sights do you want to see? What time of year are you looking to travel? What level of difficulty are you ready to tackle?

These are all questions you need to ask yourself before figuring out where you'd like to go. The time of year itself may disqualify some of your possibilities. For instance, I really wanted to ride around Italy, until I was told that Italy was going to be hotter than the hinges of hell during the time I was looking to travel. All of a sudden, Switzerland started looking fabulous.

In addition to a general sense of the country or area you want to visit, consider whether or not you want to bike in major cities or explore quieter, less-traveled areas. There is something to be said for both, as well as tours that can accommodate both, so read through the trip itineraries thoroughly and decide what sounds like the most fun.

When traveling by bike, you might also be able to eliminate some possible locations based on terrain. Sure, you might really want to see a particular place, but if that place is covered with hills, you will also be getting a personal tour of their local hospitals, which is probably not exactly the sightseeing you were hoping to get in. Be gentle with yourself when you are reading up on the difficulty levels of different rides. Remember, this is *vacation,* not a qualifying event of some sort.

Who

There are several *who's* to consider when planning your trip, and each of them will impact your overall vacation experience.

WHO WILL YOU TRAVEL WITH?

There are quite a few companies throughout the United States and the world that cater specifically to people wanting to spend their precious vacations days nursing a sore butt. (I wonder about people sometimes.) It's hard deciding what tour company to go with, because you are talking about your precious time off, and a vacation spent riding a bike could go poorly if it's not with the right group.

The best way to decide on a company is word of mouth. Ask around to see if anyone you know either has gone on a cycling trip or perhaps knows someone who has. They will be a great source of information regarding touring companies and your trip in general.

If you don't happen to hang out with people who vacation on two wheels, you can use the Internet to research your options. The website www.biketour-reviews.com has quite a bit of helpful information, as well as reviews and descriptions of many of the tour companies out there.

WHO DO THEY CATER TO?

Unless you choose a self-guided tour, you will be spending your vacation with a group of other travelers. I personally am a big fan of group travel because I like meeting new people, but it's important to know what kind of people to expect in your group. Of course, there are no set criteria for every single person who will travel with each company, but companies do cater to certain audiences.

When I was researching possible tours, I specifically chose a company that seemed to cater to a thirtysomething crowd, and that addressed the fact that it commonly had single travelers on its trips. I was taking off to spend a week with a bunch of strangers, and I really didn't want to be the only one coming to the group alone.

Group size is also an important consideration, as the number of people on the trip will definitely influence the overall dynamics. Don't be too scared of large groups, however, because they usually break up into smaller groups for each day's ride. You most likely won't be traveling with a mass of fifteen cyclists through the small village streets of a foreign land. I personally like larger groups, just because it increases your odds of not killing your fellow travelers. It can sometimes be a difficult thing to spend a week solid with complete strangers. (I can think of only a handful of good friends I'd actually want to spend a week solid with.) A smaller group can greatly heighten any personality differences, whereas a larger group limits your exposure to any one or two people and can keep things from turning into a bad *Real World* episode.

WHO WILL BE LEADING YOU?

Your trip guides will play an important role in your overall experience. On the whole, people who choose to spend their time leading other people around on bikes are usually pretty laid-back, fun people. But in addition to being fun, your guides can really enhance your trip on an informational level. If you have guides who are familiar with the area you are visiting, you will not only be led *through* your route but also be informed *about* your route. It's cool to take in all the sights, but it's also pretty neat to have some historical or cultural information to go along with what you see.

Often the information your guides have is the kind that you learn only from spending a lot of time in a particular area and getting to know it and its intricacies on a personal level. On my trip, more often than not this hard-won information led to the best food in the area. I'm sure there are other things, like facts and figures, that were shared as well, but I was too busy eating six-course meals to pay much attention.

Find out what sort of qualifications and language abilities your tour guides will have, and make sure they line up with what you think you're going to want from your trip.

How

If you are going on a cycling trip, you understand that you are signing up to travel by bike around some new land. That much is clear. But there are actually a lot of options regarding *how* you might go about it. There are many different companies that offer bike tours, and they all go about conducting them in slightly different ways. The two *hows* to take into consideration are: (1) How Are You Going to Bike? and (2) How Are You Going to Sleep? The good news is that the "How Are You Going to Eat?" question is pretty much the same on every trip—by stuffing as much food as possible into your face every night at dinner.

HOW ARE YOU GOING TO BIKE?

The different bike touring companies have varying styles of rides that range from completely independent touring to insanely "I'll just ride along beside you in this truck in case you need anything" supported trips. Before you can decide what company to go with, it's important that you figure out where your preferences fall on that scale. Would you feel comfortable with just being given a route sheet and a pat on the back before heading out on your day's ride? Or do you feel like you need a little more guidance, and maybe even the security of knowing there is a van wandering the route throughout the day, ready to help you if you need assistance (or a ride to the nearest gelato stand ASAP)?

When planning my trip, I chose to go with one of the less assisted, less structured companies and realized about halfway into my trip that perhaps I'm a little higher maintenance than I've given myself credit for. It turns out that I sorta like following a leader and not putting much thought into where I'm going or how I'm getting there. While on vacation, I'd prefer that other people do all the thinking for me while I simply nod and take another bite of chocolate and/or cheese. Luckily for me, I was able to find some leader types on the trip with me who allowed me to follow them around for a week, so it all worked out fine.

When researching companies, you'll find that some have a pretty detailed description of how their rides are conducted, while others are very vague. If you find a company that you're interested in, make sure you ask it to describe what a typical day is like on its tours. There is no right or wrong answer to this, but it will help you make your choice and avoid an unpleasant surprise when you show up for the first ride to find a map drawn only in crayon taped to your handlebars.

HOW ARE YOU GOING TO SLEEP?

Another trip feature that varies wildly by company are the accommodations. On some trips you'll be setting up camp (as in tents, for the love of God) every night, while others will lead you to five-star hotels for your slumber. Why anyone would want to ride a bike all day and then sleep on the ground at night is beyond my level of comprehension, but if that's your thing (some might point out that your "vacation" is frighteningly similar to the "life" of a homeless person, if they weren't as sensitive as I am), there are plenty of companies out there that cater to your bizarre distaste for walls. On the other hand, if you require things to be a little more fancy, you can find companies that guarantee four- or five-star hotels throughout the trip. Some tours, like the one I went on, fall somewhere in between, with stops at small local hotels that are a little off the beaten track. This is a good way to sleep in a good bed every night without feeling too prissy about your housing requirements.

Companies are usually very specific about their accommodations in their trip descriptions, so you should have no trouble narrowing down your choices to only the companies that meet your desires.

Packing

The issue of packing comes down to personal choice. Depending on how you choose to travel, you will have more than one option available to you with regard to transporting your necessities. Some people go all out and carry all of their things with them on their bike in panier bags that hang over the back tire. They are true "touring" cyclists, and God love them for their self-reliance. I am not a true anything involving physical exertion, so, needless to say, I did not carry all my stuff with me on my bike. I did, however, carry several souvenirs and some potato chips, which honestly were all I really needed.

Unless you are doing a self-guided tour, I don't recommend carrying everything with you on your bike. It will weigh you down, making your ride more difficult; it will also limit the amount of stuff you can bring with you on your trip. Most tour groups have baggage transfer options either already included in their prices or available for an extra fee. I ended up paying the extra fee to have my luggage moved from location to location because I have a packing disability that leaves me unable to ever pack less than fifty pounds for any trip (doctors are working diligently on a cure), and I felt like that weight may turn my road bike into a stationary bike rather quickly.

If you are like me and you end up on a bike tour in a faraway land, and you are doing it for the fun of it, for the beauty of it, for a vacation, then load up your suitcase with everything you would for any other vacation (if your other vacations included padded shorts) and pay the extra fee to have some poor soul drag it from stop to stop. One thing to remember while loading up is that you are on a vacation first and a bike second. Yes, most of your packing will be bike-centric, but don't forget to throw in a couple sets of street clothes as well. Once you get to your stopping point every day, you may still want to go out and explore, and doing so in bike shorts can make you a bit of an eyesore on the classic beauty of your vacation spot. Also, pack a few nice dinner outfits so you can sample the local cuisine at night without feeling out of place.

I offer you one small rule as the most important thing to remember when it comes to packing: Do not pack anything that still has the tag on it. Or anything that you just ripped the tag off of. I know you are going on vacation and you are running around town with your to-pack list, buying up all the bike goodies you need to be a successful bike tourist. But you are going to be considerably less successful if the first time you try out everything on your to-pack list is after you unpack it from your suitcase after your arrival. Just like you would in a long road race, it's important that you tackle your bike tour with the things you are already used to. This will decrease the chances of major discomfort (unless, like me, it's *gigantic* hills that define the word "discomfort").

The actual items you pack will depend on where and when you are going. Consult your tour company for recommendations on appropriate clothing. Just remember that you don't need a new, cute biking outfit for each day of your trip. You are going to be cycling for the majority of your day, so being cute is sort of off your possibilities list. And that's okay, because it's off everyone else's list as well, so at least you'll all look terrible together. Eventually, you'll actually forget that you've been wearing the same outfit for four days and that you look roughly like you've been run over by a herd of cattle. Fast-moving cattle. Who somehow spilled wine on you. Your appearance will become evident only after you get your trip pictures back, but that is why God invented photo-editing software.

I know this seems like a lot of information to take in, but the more details you work out before you travel across the globe, the better your overall globe-traveling experience will be in the long run (or long ride, as it were).

One last piece of advice about going on a bike tour involves actually getting on your bike before the tour. Most touring companies offer different route options each day, ranging in mileage from easy to difficult. This will give you a little bit of leeway if you aren't feeling up to a huge ride every day. But even on the easy rides you are still going to have to do some actual riding. (Bummer, right? I know, I was sort of hoping to just get a picture with me holding my bike over my head on the first day and then spend the rest of the vacation catching some rays.) While you don't have to be an elite cyclist in order to enjoy a bike tour, you really should do your best to spend some time on a bike before you go. Get out for at least a few longer rides before you take off on vacation. This will give your body a little advance warning of what is to come and allow it to prepare itself accordingly. You don't want to be getting used to riding a bike on the first few days of your trip. Believe you me, getting used to sitting on a bike for hours at a time is not something that goes hand in hand with a good-time vacation.

Ride for Fun

One of my favorite things about cyclists is that they tend to be a pretty good-natured group of people. Sure, they enjoy spending their free time in spandex and funny-sounding shoes, but I don't hold that against them. Overall, you'll find that people who engage in athletic activities regularly seem to have a pretty good sense of humor about their activity of choice, and are usually down for mixing a little fun into their sport.

You will be spending a lot of your training doing really unfun things, like trying to avoid heart explosion while pedaling up a ninety-degree incline or sticking your hands down your pants in public to apply Butt Butter to your crotch. To lessen these training traumas, it's important to seek out the fun aspects of your new sport. The best way to find out about fun times is to hang out with people who cycle regularly. They are in the know when it comes to fun events involving their sport (and they can probably give you some public-crotch-rubbing tips, too).

Below, I've listed some of the more interesting events I've come across. They are merely a few of the random things people decide to do while riding bikes, and I hope they inspire you to be a little more random in your bike-riding adventures.

TOUR DE DONUT
Texas (www.tourdedonut.com)
Illinois (www.bebikeclub.com/tourdedonut)
Finally, an event I can get behind. Basically, anything with the word "donut" in the name is something I want to be a part of.

This ride is like any other ride, but with the fantastic addition of donuts. Cyclists complete the thirty-mile ride and get five minutes off their time for every donut they consume along the way. Many end up with "negative time," which means they consumed more than six donuts. These people are true warriors.

When visiting the website for this ride, I came across a cyclist who summed up the event like this: "Eat as many donuts as you can without throwing up." As I watched a video of one participant pushing three donuts together and shoving them into his mouth, I realized I've been training for this ride for my entire life.

CRITICAL MASS

www.critical-mass.info (also, many local affiliates can be found on MySpace and/or Facebook)

Critical Mass started in 1992 as a political statement of sorts. San Francisco cyclists wanted to stake their claim on city roads and felt that a large quantity of bikes on those roads at the same time might begin to make their point. Since then, Critical Mass groups have been started all over the country and the world. Rides are usually held on the last Friday of the month and are not organized in any way other than there usually being a predetermined time and meeting place. At that time, a bunch of cyclists take off together along city streets, making their presence known.

These rides have angered local authorities in many areas because they often disrupt traffic and cause headaches for police. The police would prefer that Critical Mass riders apply for the appropriate permits before taking to the streets en masse, but it seems like that would be sort of against the whole point of taking to the streets en masse.

Depending on what city you live in, these rides can be quite huge and well worth checking out. You'll get in some miles and be a rabble-rouser at the same time—a fun way to spend a Friday afternoon, if you ask me. Just try not to get arrested. Going to the county jail in spandex can't be a good idea.

MOONLIGHT RAMBLE, ST. LOUIS

www.moonlightramble.com/mr/home.html

This is one of many midnight rides that happen all over the country. This particular one boasts over ten thousand riders, which sounds like a crazy-good time in the middle of the night. Events like this aren't going to help you get much exercise, but they are a great way to connect with your fellow cyclists and to experience a unique biking event.

TOUR DE FAT

www.tour-de-fat.com

There doesn't seem to be much actual cycling involved in the event, but the amount of beer involved quickly makes you forget that you aren't actually riding your bike at a bike event.

Tour de Fat is a festival of sorts that sets up shop in eleven cities throughout the United States and encourages people to live a more bike-centric life. They start out with a parade of wildly decorated bikes and end with a fundraiser that features much beer and music. The money raised goes to local biketastic nonprofit organizations. So it's all for a good cause, even if that cause has nothing to do with actually riding your bike. Yay, philanthropy!

WORLD NAKED BIKE RIDE

www.worldnakedbikeride.org

This ride is pretty self-explanatory. Good news: no spandex! Bad news: It turns out the spandex were covering your private areas.

The point of this ride (besides getting some awesome Christmas card photos) is to protest the world's dependence on oil. Riders believe that bicycles present a wonderful alternative to automobiles and therefore could save the world from its oil addiction. I'm not entirely sure what the nudity has to do with oil. But it sounds messy.

Drinking and Biking

Although this is not a legal or recommended activity, I feel like I should point out the abundance of drinking-centered bike events out there. It seems every time I start talking to cyclists about fun events, the conversation inevitably leads to "I've heard of this one ride where people ride all around the city, drinking their way from one bar to another." Or sometimes they are a little more involved: "This one ride, it starts at 3:00 AM in a parking garage; then you ride for ten miles, drinking the whole time. People are pulling kegs behind them, and the main goal is to keep drinking and never stop riding. It's not easy staying on a bike while pumping a keg."

Again, none of this is legal, and I would not recommend that you break the law, mostly because then you would probably sue me. But you should be well aware that this cycling world is full of lushes. I'm not sure how one pulls a keg behind their bike, but it might be something worth checking out if you want to hang out with the cool kids.

Eppie's Not-So-Great Race

This weekend I participated in my first organized event on my bike. It was a triathlon, of which I did one of the -athlons. My friend Michaela has been doing triathlons the past couple of years and has gotten all fit and trim and enamored with three activities in one event. A few weeks ago she was talking about Eppie's Great Race, a popular local triathlon that happens every year. The three legs of the race are running, biking, and kayaking. When she asked me if I wanted to do the race with her, I told her that I'm more of a uni-athalon sort of girl. I'm biking right now and couldn't possibly be expected to engage in any other activity.

It turns out you can enter the race as a team, so Michaela offered to take on running and kayaking, while I tore apart the cycling. This made for some interesting logistics because the cycling was the second leg of the triathlon. That meant that poor Michaela had to run, then get picked up in a car and taken to the end of my cycling route so that she could start her kayaking. With all the people participating in the race, and all the traffic getting to and from every leg, it took a while for Michaela to get from the end of the running to the beginning of the kayaking.

This would have probably been a tight fit if Michaela were doing the race with anyone besides me. But since I was the one doing the cycling leg, she had plenty of time to get to her next stop. She even had time to unload the kayak, get it ready, get changed into kayaking clothes, and grab a beverage. I'm pretty sure she might have caught a little catnap, too. That's how slow I was.

>>>

It wasn't until I started my leg of the race that I discovered how slow I am. There's nothing quite like surrounding yourself with other athletes to make you realize exactly where you fall on the competency scale. I'll give you a hint: Look for me toward the bottom of that scale. I started getting passed almost immediately after I embarked on my twelve-mile ride. And not just passed, but abandoned. I was left for dead while the other cyclists sped off into the distance, not in my sight for longer than about twenty seconds before they were so far ahead of me that I couldn't see them anymore.

My mom, ever the comedian, gave me a mug the other day that said I'M SO FAR BEHIND, I THOUGHT I WAS IN 1ST PLACE. That mug would be alarmingly true (and sorta mean-spirited under the circumstances), except it's impossible to think you're in first place when you've been passed roughly 8,456,453 times.

It's becoming somewhat ridiculous how horrible I am at every friggin' sport I decide to take on. It's starting to give me a complex. It's not like I have any real excuse for my complete lack of endurance and athletic abilities. I'm not overweight, I'm relatively young, my body doesn't have any major deformities (my middle toes on both my feet *are* a little long), and I was a total tomboy as a kid. I don't throw like a girl, I can kick a soccer ball fifty yards with no problem, and I can hold my own at a game of HORSE. And yet I am simply not good at sports I tackle as an adult. I spent the better part of my marathon training being lapped by sixty-five-year-old women who were *walking,* and now it seems I'm destined for a similar fate in the cycling world (those sixty-five-year-old walkers are quick). What's wrong with me?

>>>

I feel like I'm doing everything right. I mean, I'm pedaling, I'm pushing, I'm breathing, I bought Lance Armstrong's book. And yet people are just *whizzing* by me as though I am standing still. They can't *all* be taking performance-enhancing drugs, so it's gotta be something else. Skill, perhaps? Maybe strength? Or attitude? Hmmmm.

I gotta get me some drugs.

My Ears

If my general lack of athletic prowess and overall disdain for movement weren't enough of a handicap in my cycling efforts, it turns out that my *actual* handicap is kind of an issue as well.

I'm hearing impaired and wear hearing aids to, well, aid in my hearing. When I was training for a marathon, I'd take my ears out simply because I was sweating roughly twelve gallons a minute from my head and didn't want to experiment with my electronic devices' tolerance for liquids. But in cycling I don't sweat nearly as much, and I actually enjoy being able to hear what is going on around me, so I leave my ears in.

This poses a bit of an issue, though, since my hearing aids are basically just microphones in my ears. Have you heard what it sounds like when a microphone tries to pick up sound in the wind? *Vrrrrusssshhhhhhmmmmmkkkkkrrrssshhhhhh* is a rough interpretation. When I am riding my bike, the air is whizzing by me, creating a windlike phenomenon. Which

>>>

leads to really annoying, hurricanelike sounds in my head the entire time I'm riding.

The only way to avoid those sounds is to turn my head at a ninety-degree angle and basically look to the side the whole time I'm riding (which is highly recommended cycling form, any pro will tell you). And even then, I'm not able to hear much except the person riding directly beside me. That would be okay, if the person directly beside me were the only person speaking to me. Unfortunately, that's usually not the case.

Out on the bike trail and in road races, cyclists let you know when they are coming up to pass you by saying, "On your left." This lets you know they are there and will be, in a moment's time, on your left, and then, in one more moment's time, in front of you. And then way in front of you and then eventually finished with their ride while you are still pedaling away weakly, continuing to be passed by more and more cyclists. Not that I have a complex or anything.

Anyhoo, I've had to take to riding as close to the right edge of the bike trail as possible because I can never actually hear the "on your lefts" and instead end up hearing a lot of "Look out!" or "Wake up!" as I accidentally come too close to a passing rider.

One of the more unfortunate side effects of this hurricane in my head is the fact that I feel the need to scream over it when I'm talking. You'd think I wouldn't be under the impression that the hurricane is occurring someplace other than just in my head, and others can hear it as well, but, well. . . . This means that my conversations involve a lot of yelling on my part, which isn't a huge deal—except when

I am screaming things that perhaps the whole outdoors doesn't need to hear.

The other day, while pedaling along, I felt the need to articulate, with great class, what I was feeling at that exact moment. So I let loose with *"My hoo-ha hurts!"* My riding partner, Sarah, just smiled and shook her head. A millisecond later, a man passed us on his bike, newly informed of my general discomfort and dissatisfaction with my hoo-ha. "Inappropriate, on your right," I mumbled.

New York, Day 1

After my peaceful journey through the Swiss Alps, I decided that I would try a slight change of pace with the NYC Century Bike Tour. And by "slight change of pace," I mean the complete friggin' opposite of a peaceful journey.

Why do I do these things to myself, really?

I had been looking for a century ride, and the NYC Century seemed like a fun one. It had thousands of cyclists and would wind its way through Manhattan, Brooklyn, Queens, and the Bronx. This sounded like a cool way to see New York and an exciting way to tackle a century ride. The words "cool" and "exciting" started to fade away, though, when I found out that the ride would involve cycling one hundred miles "with traffic." "With traffic" means that the roads we would be traveling on would be open to traffic as well as bikes. That concept is not cool or exciting so much as it's scary as hell.

>>>

Not wanting to take on New York City by myself, I enlisted two friends to come on my adventure with me. Ruth, a die-hard cyclist, was also a native New Yorker, so I figured she could assist me with all of my bike problems, as well as give me someone to follow throughout the city. I was going to have enough problems navigating the busy streets of New York without trying to actually navigate where the hell I was supposed to be going at the same time.

Ruth would have to fly to New York from her home in Portland, but I knew she'd be up for the adventure. The woman will ride her bike pretty much anywhere and actually has a bike that can fold up and fit into a suitcase. It's very "Transformers, more than meets the eye" when she pulls a functioning bike out of a suitcase. She had the bike custom-made by a company called Bike Friday that has an entire business catering to people who feel like a bike in a suitcase would complete their travel experience. This seems somewhat foreign to me, seeing as a Cinnabon is the only thing I ever try to cram into my suitcase while traveling. To each her own, I guess.

Ruth and I were also joined by our friend Sherry. Sherry has a Bike Friday bike as well, but she is not a supercyclist like Ruth. Honestly, I think she just thought it would be cool to buy a bike that she could pull out of a suitcase. It's highly probable that she'd be just as excited about pulling my Cinnabon out of a suitcase if she could get a custom-baked one with her name on it. Sherry is my kind of girl.

So the three of us descended upon the city, ready to hit the mean streets of New York while wearing padded shorts and colorful helmets. Bring it, NYC.

>>>

>>>

Our New York Bike Adventure from Hell began on a Friday evening. It was late summer/early fall, so I expected the weather to be decent. Instead, when I got into New York and was waiting for my luggage, I caught a glimpse of a weather report on a nearby TV screen. What I saw was a map of New York with a very colorful blob heading its way. Apparently, a tropical storm was moving toward the city—which seemed hugely unfortunate and unfair.

When I woke up on Saturday morning I looked outside the hotel window, half expecting to see people blowing by in the wind. Instead, everything looked peaceful and clear. So I figured maybe the storm had taken a turn and gone to drop buckets of water on other cyclists. This was great news.

Since I'd come to a different state to do a race and I couldn't fit my bike into my suitcase, I had to rent a bike for the event. I found the closest bike shop with an available road bike and headed down to rent it for the following day's event. As we walked the seven blocks to the bike shop, I discovered the joy that is New York humidity. It felt like all the huge city buildings were closing in on my lungs and pushing massive amounts of sweat out of my body at the same time. Overall, it seemed like perfect weather for a strenuous athletic event.

We made it to the bike shop, where they fitted the bike to my body, and I was ready to go. I pushed the bike outside to where Sherry was waiting for me, and I almost instantly felt my heart rate double. Cars were zipping by, honking, screeching, swerving in and out of lanes with abandon. I looked down the street to see that most of the available bike lane was filled with double-parked cars and/or open passenger doors.

>>>

>>>

"You ready to go?" Sherry asked. I clipped on my helmet and tightened it so hard that I nearly decapitated myself. "Um, yeah. There are a lot of cars."

"It's New York City. What were you expecting?"

With that, Sherry took off down the street, leaving me no other option than to follow her. Unlike hers, my bike could not fold up and fit into one of the many passing cabs, so I threw my leg over it and started pedaling in the direction of what I assumed would be my first hit-and-run police report.

Right off the bat, things did not go well. My first instinct when riding in New York was to brake. Unfortunately, when I reached down for my hand brakes on my handlebars, where I usually find them on my bike, there was nothing there. My poor fingers were left flailing in the wind, grabbing at air while trying to stop the bike. Most normal cyclists might have actually taken inventory of little things like brakes and maybe even tire pressure before leaving the store. Reason number #2348 I might not be an elite athlete. This bike's brakes were on the lower part of the handlebars, so in order to stop the bike I had to bend over and reach one hand down to the brake. This was an extremely convenient way to ride along a busy street, let me tell you.

The humidity I spoke of earlier seemed to close in on me even more with every rotation of my wheels. I could feel a trail of sweat forming and running freely between my breasts, as well as down my back. The obstructed bike lane meant I had to veer into traffic and hope that it did not veer back into me. I kept an eye on Sherry, not wanting to lose visual contact with the only person in New York who might care if I fell down a manhole. I watched as she wove recklessly in and

>>>

out of traffic, and as many large trucks came stupidly close to hitting her with their side mirrors. Each time this happened, I'd gasp and clench my eyes shut, not wanting to witness her impalement. Her reaction was a little different, however. She'd yell an obscenity and flip off the motorist, which seemed like a fantastic way to endear herself to NYC.

After the first two blocks, Sherry and I stopped at a red light and evaluated the ride thus far. "Did you see those asses honk at me?!"

"Yes, you sorta swerved into their lane."

"Where was I supposed to swerve? There were cars in the bike lane."

"How many more blocks do we have?"

"About twenty."

"Awesome."

I cinched my helmet a little tighter.

Twenty blocks later, we arrived at our destination and my blood pressure reached an all-time high. My hands were permanently attached to my handlebars, with two fingers permanently attached to my brakes, ready to squeeze at the first sign of an oncoming vehicle/person/traffic cone. The only good news was that it was starting to feel a little cooler. I had already soaked through my clothes, but the cooling temperature gave me hope for the next day's ride. This hope was short-lived, however, because minutes later the cooling temperatures became a torrential downpour. Turns out those weather maps are pretty accurate and that tropical storm actually *was* heading toward New York City. At least I wasn't hot anymore.

>>>

We still had several blocks until we got back to our hotel, and we didn't have many options besides riding our bikes. During these remaining blocks, all the good times of city riding were still there, but now I had the added bonus of not being able to see anything at all. The crazy amount of rain hitting my glasses made it pretty much impossible to see, so I took them off and was left with the horribly blurry vision that makes said glasses requisite. Shockingly, I realized that vision didn't really increase my odds of surviving New York City on a bike. With cars and people coming out of nowhere, your odds of avoiding death are only about 50/50, whether or not you can actually see your obstacles. The lack of seeing was actually kind of a relief, because I wasn't aware of all the things ahead of me that might have caused my demise.

When we finally got back to the hotel, my clothes, which only a few minutes ago had been stuck to me with sweat, were now drenched and plastered to me as though I'd just climbed out of a pool. Wearing a bike helmet. The hotel's A/C was still kicked up from the humid temperatures we'd been suffering from only thirty minutes earlier, and we all immediately went into a hypothermic state the second we reached the lobby.

So, Day 1 in New York went smashingly well. I could only imagine what wonders awaited me the next day when I actually rode farther than twenty-five blocks.

Tour de the Alps

Now that I am an expert cyclist, I decided that the next logical step would be for me to take a cycling vacation. Because that's what athletes do: They plan vacations around body movement and sweating. (The only sweating I usually do on vacation is when I occasionally sprint toward the all-you-can-eat buffet.) Once I made the decision to go on a cycling trip, I started researching my options by Googling "bike vacations" and was quite surprised by how many companies cater to those who can think of no better way to spend their time away from work than getting involved in an activity that risks hamstring injuries. I'm always amazed, when venturing into the athletic world, to find out how many people are already there, burning calories left and right, without my ever having noticed them throughout my sedentary life. What have I been doing with my life that I've never heard anything about cycling vacations? I guess cycling tour companies don't advertise at Taco Bell.

Shortly after I began my search for my perfect cycling adventure in faraway lands, my aunt handed me a magazine that featured a article written by a woman who had gone on her own bike adventure in Italy with a company called Blue Marble. Blue Marble wasn't as swanky as other bike tour companies, and it seemed to take a laid-back approach to travel. The writer described a wonderful trip surrounded by the beauty and tastes of Italy, as well as a newfound bond with her grown son, who'd accompanied her on the trip. The article made cycling through Europe sound extremely poetic

>>>

and life-altering, with very little mention of butt soreness or exhaustion.

I was so inspired by this article that I immediately went to the Blue Marble website to find my next vacation. As I looked around the site, I found it disarmingly low-tech and quite confusing to navigate. But I was convinced that this was intentional, and I didn't want to go on a foo-foo trip with some company that catered to an upscale clientele who'd be impressed by things like graphic design and logical website navigation. I was going on an adventure! Adventures aren't upscale! If they were, the people on the Discovery Channel would look a lot more put together.

I inquired with Blue Marble about going to Italy on my own life-altering adventure, similar to that of the woman who'd written the inspiring article. But I was told that Italy was going to be insanely hot during the time I was looking to travel, so I turned my sights to other possible life-altering countries. I'd heard great things about the Swiss and their chocolates, so I signed up for a tour through the Swiss Alps. One might question why I signed up for a bike tour with the word "Alps" in it, but then one might be underestimating my affection for good chocolate.

I couldn't convince anyone else that cycling through the Alps was a good use of their time and money (apparently, you can actually buy Swiss chocolate right at your local grocery store, so a lot of my friends weren't that impressed with my promise of sweets), so I was on my own in heading off to explore a faraway land. The trip would include other bikers in a group travel setting, which I was looking forward to. Many people do not enjoy traveling with groups of strangers, but to me it sounded ideal.

Meeting up with new people who are drawn to the same kind of trip as you are is a really cool way to meet travelers from all over the world whom you would otherwise never come into contact with. It is definitely a risky venture, because there's no way to tell if you are going to be sharing your vacation with people who will drive you insane and cause you to want to impale them with one of your souvenirs, but I figure that traveling with friends always runs the exact same risk. I've met some of my most favorite people on the planet through group travel, so I'm always up for these types of trips.

I flew off to Switzerland and arrived what felt like twelve days later. My trip involved several flights (one of them missed), an eight-hour delay in Paris, an overnight stay in Italy, and a random train adventure into Switzerland. All of this happened in countries where I spoke not a lick of the local language, which made the adventure that much more fun and not that frustrating at all. When I finally arrived at my destination, I realized that Blue Marble hadn't given me any details regarding meeting up with my group leader, other than "meet at dinnertime." "Dinnertime" seemed like a less-than-specific time to have international travelers hook up with a tour guide.

I emailed the Blue Marble home office from my hotel room after I checked in to ask the all-important question: What time was I supposed to meet up with my tour guide? The response? "Dinnertime." Yeah. So that was helpful. Instead of randomly wandering the streets, looking for someone I didn't know and who didn't know me, I stayed in my room and waited for someone to figure out I was there. I thought perhaps the whole checking-in-under-my-name thing might have been a good clue as to my whereabouts. But about five hours later, there was a knock at my door and a confused man standing on the other side. "We didn't know you were here." Hmmm. This was when I started to realize that perhaps foo-foo might have been a better way to go.

On our first day I met my fellow travelers: a couple, David and Dena, from D.C.; a single mother, Amber, from Los Angeles; and an older dentist, Howard, from a small town in Pennsylvania. We made an interesting group, albeit a small one. It turns out the economy and the weak U.S. dollar were keeping quite a few people away from Europe this summer, which meant a much smaller group than normal for a Blue Marble trip. Over breakfast I learned that David, Dena, and Howard had all been on cycling trips before, and that Amber had been inspired by the very same article that had prompted my trip. It was comforting to know there was someone else on the tour who was as eager to abandon all sense of reason.

We were all given a route sheet with directions on how to navigate around the countryside for the day. We learned that our tour guide, Marcus, wasn't going to be guiding us so much as he'd be waiting for a while after we left and then following behind us to make sure we were okay. I was a bit intimidated by the combination of my lack of language skills and the lack of detailed directions on the route sheet. These concerns were eased slightly when Howard and Amber said we could all ride together. This was great news, because they both seemed like people who enjoyed being leaders and I was mostly looking forward to following for the duration of the trip. Looking for street signs is hard work, and I was on vacation.

David and Dena took off first, geared up to the max, complete with two wireless earpieces that were apparently going to allow them to speak to each other while they rode. It was very Secret Service of them. Howard, Amber, and I took off in a different direction, opting for the shorter route. We were not geared up and felt no need to be superstars on our first day out. We zipped through tiny Swiss streets in the cutest town ever. The air was cool and the landscape lush. Then, after two miles, we came across a stupidly big hill. This was a more-than-unfortunate way to start the day. I pedaled hard and slowly, trying not to pass out within the first hour of my vacation. At one point I had to stop and get off my bike, afraid that I might get sick if I kept pedaling. It was at this point that I realized why no one wanted to come on this trip with me. Who spends their vacation bent over on the side of the road, gasping for breath? That would be me, thank you very much.

After what seemed like forever, I finally made it to the top of the Hill from Hell. Even though I'd encouraged them to go on without me, Amber and Howard were at the top, waiting patiently for me to finish my climb. How sweet were these two, waiting for a complete stranger to lug herself up to meet them? The warm feeling brought on by their considerate nature almost overshadowed the burning feeling in my lungs. Almost.

We rode for a little while longer, through open land with lush farms and trees. Everywhere we looked it was like another postcard photo—at a certain point I had to stop stopping for

>>>

every cool photo op because I was doing more photographing than riding (not that I minded that much).

Perhaps because of these delays, our tour guide caught up to us not far into our ride. We were just experiencing our first big downhill—our reward for the Hill from Hell—when Marcus came coasting by. He made sure everything was okay and then said he'd meet us at the bottom of the hill. Then off he went, as fast as his wheels would take him, arms outstretched, looking like he could possibly take flight. This experience was clearly filed under "job perks" for this young man.

By the time we met up with him at the bottom of the hill, we had crossed over into France. Marcus led us into a small French village, where we ate at an even smaller Irish pub. It was all very international of us. We ate the first of the trip's many cheese-centered meals, a meal that involved wine as well. The Blue Marble groups enjoy their wine about as much as they enjoy their bikes. And I'm pretty sure they enjoy their bikes mainly because that is how they get to the wine.

Before the trip I wasn't much of a drinker, especially of wine. It's an acquired taste that I never acquired, and therefore it tasted horrible to me. But if an Irish pub in France while on a bike tour isn't a great place to start drinking wine, I really don't know what is. And so began my biking/drinking tour of Switzerland and France. Things were looking up.

After lunch we wound through even more countryside and into some other tiny towns with old architecture that nearly looked fake because it was so cute. I pulled up next to a beautiful church, leaned my bike against a stone wall, and went inside. It was empty and quiet, the way I prefer my churches. The others followed me in, and we each sat at a

>>>

pew, silently absorbing the beauty of the building and what it meant to the many people who seek refuge there.

After our spiritual awakening, we continued on for many miles, winding and climbing, in and out of populated and open spaces. Just as we were about to cross back over into Switzerland, we came across a street fair of sorts, so we stopped to check it out. (I could definitely get used to cycling with this many stops.)

The street fair had trinkets galore and was basically a huge garage sale, but as we wandered around I thought I heard familiar music coming from nearby. I recognized the tune, but the words were in a different language. As we made our way to the other side of the fair, we were greeted by a mass of people wearing cowboy hats and boots, dancing to the stylings of a French country-western band. The dancers were boot-scootin' boogying to decade-old American country songs. It was awesome. "Are we really watching line dancing in the middle of a French street fair right now?" asked Amber. I couldn't answer because I was too busy singing along to John Michael Montgomery at the top of my lungs.

Marcus asked Amber to two-step, and they danced just outside the mass of line dancers, wearing spandex and covered in sweat. Because why not add one more random thing to this scenario?

We made it back into Switzerland that night in time for a wonderful meal made even more wonderful by the amount of miles we'd ridden that day. Food takes on hints of ecstasy when following physical activity, I've found. We didn't even mind when we missed our train back to the hotel and had to walk a mile or so in the dark. It was along a beautiful lake, which reflected the million stars in the sky. A peaceful end to a beautiful first day.

The rest of the trip was similar to the first day: lots of riding and plenty of stops to eat and drink. One day we actually stopped for a snack of cheese, wine, bread, prosciutto, and fruit a mere ten minutes before we stopped for lunch. Eating was a priority, you see. Especially because the food was so damn good. I'd order based on suggestions every night because I was not able to read the French on the menus. And every night the food was amazing, even though most of the time I didn't know exactly what it was I was eating. Somehow my stomach, which usually doesn't fit much in it, was more than happy to accommodate four-course meals. "Dessert?" Answer: "Always."

We rode our way in and out of Switzerland and France by bike, train, and boat. One day I was mountain biking down an alp at the highest elevation imaginable; other days I rode on a path that seemed to cut through the Alps, with mountains jutting up on all sides of me. We ate fruit off orchard trees and cheese from an actual cheese museum. I spun around like Maria von Trapp on a flowered mountainside, while the others sang, "The hills are alive with the sound of muuuuuuusic." I danced in a fountain and took photos as our guide jumped off a high dive into Lake Geneva. We ate an apple in a town named Apple and chocolate in every other town.

Although I took only one spill over my handlebars, my legs were covered in bruises that made me look like I'd lost a bar fight (albeit a bar fight with a midget). They didn't hurt, but maybe the wine helped in that regard. And the chocolate probably had some sort of medicating elements as well.

>>>

We saw the places we traversed in ways we never could have via any other form of transportation. And I came to respect the bike as something far more than just a form of exercise. What other athletic pastime could take us through the hundreds of miles we covered? We rode and rode, breathing in the air of this foreign land, the smells and the wind brushing our faces. When we wanted to stop for a picture (every four minutes) or a drink (every 2.5 minutes) or just to touch something, we would simply pedal over, hop off our bikes, and do it. There was nothing complicated about it—no parking to find; no loading everyone in and out of a bus.

We'd go off the route sheets, sometimes by accident, and yet always find our way to the end point somehow. (And by "we" I mean that other people who actually read the route sheets found our way to the end.) It wasn't a huge deal and just ended up adding to the adventure of it all.

As for the adventure, I'm not sure it is for everyone. There is very little structure; time becomes *time ranges,* directions become *however you manage to get there.* Our group was small, but I imagine a group much bigger would run into quite a few logistical issues. You have to be a certain type of person to be able to go with the flow of group travel even when things aren't flowing so well. I like to think of myself as that type of person, but every once in a while I'd realize I'm more high maintenance than I give myself credit for. Perhaps next time I'll go with a more foo-foo group. I've heard they have wine and cheese waiting for you at the end of your ride every day. I could go with that flow.

But on this trip, in this place, I got what I had come for: not quite a life-changing journey, but surely a unique one, and

>>>

>>>

a new way to see the world, a new part of the world to see. All because a few months ago I got on a bike and started spinning around my neighborhood a little. I could never have imagined what I'd see while on those two wheels. I can't wait to see where they take me next.

The Hills

Oh, the hills of Switzerland.

Considering I was in the friggin' Alps, the routes we took were surprisingly flat. We climbed all the huge mountains via train, not bike, which was lovely. But there were still some hills and I still had to find a way up them. Each time I swore my legs and/or lungs weren't going to survive the climb, but then, miraculously, they did. After each climb came the fall—breathtakingly fast descents into waiting valleys. The promise of a downhill on the other side was what pushed me through the climbs.

It all became quite metaphorical, as things tend to become when you are pushing your physical limits. Life, I thought, is a lot like these hills. Sometimes you are at points when the effort seems too great, the obstacles too high. And then, even though you never thought you'd make it, you do. And after that, just when you are starting to breathe correctly, just when you are thanking the Lord for a little relief, is when the descents start.

>>>

>>>

Beautiful, rushing descents are as close as I'll ever come to flying while actually still being connected to the ground. You are moving so fast, with such freedom, and it's all so *easy.* Just a moment ago you were gasping for breath, barely trudging forward with the waning strength of your tired legs, but now you are flying with no effort at all.

The flying is amazing, but the tricky part, the part that keeps so many from ever getting to that bliss, is that you have to climb first. There is no freedom without struggle. Sure, the flat lands are pretty and can make you content, but they aren't where the rush is. That can be found only just beyond the moment when you think you've had enough. And then, like an answer, comes the descent.

CHAPTER *four*
The Big Event

t's heeeeeere, the big event. Are you so excited? And perhaps a little nauseous, too? God, I love sports.

I know that you've worked for a long time preparing for this event, and you are probably rather nervous about how you are going to fare. The most important thing to remember when heading into your century ride is that all those random rides you've been doing the past few months weren't really that random at all. There was an actual rhyme and reason to those endless miles. So even though your mind is nervous about your event, your body is actually quite prepared. At this point, your body no longer even shudders when you throw a stupid amount of miles in front of it. So really, the only thing left for you to do is to show up at the start line and get started on your one last ride. (The last ride of your training schedule, I mean—not of, like, your *whole life*. That would be a bit dramatic.)

Before you head out on that final voyage, there are a few things you should make note of. As you can see by looking at your training schedule, the week before your event is filled with a whole lot of tapering, and you will therefore have a little extra time on your hands. While I highly recommend spending that time doing as little as possible (that's what "tapering" means, right?), you should do a couple things to make sure you're all set on race day.

Before

First of all, go ahead and make sure you actually registered for the event you think you're doing in five days. Sometimes little things like registering can get lost when you are spending all your free time icing your crotch and cursing the inventors of the bike seat. If you did register for your event, the organizers of said event might have sent you some general event information, along with your race number and route map. Take a look over all of this info and familiarize yourself with all the details of your event, include start time and place. Those two facts will prove to be quite helpful in your racing efforts. If you didn't get any race materials from the event itself, don't freak out. It's likely they will have all your details available for pickup on race day. Jump on the event website and find out if this is the case, or if perhaps all the info you need is simply available for download. You're gonna want to do all of this at the beginning of the week so that you have time to figure out any problems or questions that come up. The morning of the event is not the time to figure them out.

You want your bike to be in tip-top shape for your ride, so take it in for a tune-up the week before your race day. This will ease your mind about the health of your bike, and since you will be spending that week pretty much avoiding your two-wheeled metal friend, you won't even notice its absence (what you will notice is an unfamiliar feeling of joy and relaxation—savor it).

Carbo-loading is another thing to put on the to-do list for your precentury week. The good news is, I'm pretty sure you can combine this with lying on the couch, so it shouldn't be that hard to fit it in. The key to carbo-loading is that you need to do it for about three days before your ride. You can't load adequately in just one day. A lot of people have a big, carb-heavy meal the night before their big race, and that is fine. But in addition to that, you are going to need to be building up your glycogen levels (good stuff), and carbs are the way to do that (better stuff). Throughout your training, you've been making carbs about 60–65 percent of your food intake. During your few days of carb heaven, you are going to need to up that by about 10 percent. Just submerge yourself in a vat of cookie dough. That ought to work.

The night before your event (when you get a brief break from stuffing pasta in your face), get all of your race stuff together in an orderly pile. Check and double-check your list of necessities before you go to bed (use my handy list in Appendix A). You are most likely going to be climbing out of bed in the middle of the farkin' night to embark on your big race day, and if you're anything like me, mornings aren't a great time for you to organize. Get as much stuff done as you can the night before, so all you have to do is roll out of bed and onto your bike in the morning. Sure, sleeping with your helmet on might not be that comfortable, but dammit, it's foolproof.

The morning of the race, you should eat a nice-size breakfast a few hours before you hit the start line. This might not always be a feasible option, because of the craziness of race day, but absolutely eat something, because without that breakfast, things could go bad pretty quickly in the race.

During

The only things you really have to remember when doing your actual ride are the many things you've done on all your other rides. The whole point of your training program was to train your body and to train yourself on the best way to finish long rides. Don't do anything crazy on this ride. Stick to the things that proved successful (anything that didn't cause you to vomit and/or cry) during your training. Eat food you know agrees with your stomach, and keep a pace you know won't cause cardiac arrest.

Speaking of pace, try not to get too excited at the beginning and head out at a faster pace than you are used to. (The beginning of a race always involves moving and mornings, so I never had to worry about getting too excited, but not everyone can be as strong as me.) If anything, aim to take the first half of your ride a little more slowly than might feel comfortable. Sometimes when you are riding with a group of people on race day, you can suddenly find yourself wiped out at mile 30 because you've unknowingly been pushing yourself too hard in an effort to keep up with them and the excitement of the race. If you do want to ride with other cyclists, try to pick a group whose pace you're comfortable with. The benefit of riding with a group is to help motivate you along, not completely knock you out. If you feel like pushing yourself a little harder as the race rolls on, then do so in tiny increments—nothing too drastic all at once.

Organized races will have rest stops along the way that offer various foods, beverages, bathrooms, massages, and entertainment (mostly in the vein of watching people see how much food they can hold in their arms and shove in their mouths at the same time). Stop at each of these stops and engage in all it has to offer. Especially the food. It is important that you keep yourself fueled along your ride, and you can do so by snacking on the food you brought along with you, but why not get off the saddle for a few minutes (or more) and load up on free goodies? Somehow, free food is always exciting—it's just human nature—and you're going to need to take excitement wherever you can get it during long-distance events. Be careful not to get too excited and eat yourself sick, though, since that would lead to things that aren't so exciting at all.

After

Now that you've made it across the finish line, you are officially ready for a party and a nap, not necessarily in that order. While you figure out the order, you're going to want to replenish your body with the many things you've emptied out of it over the last several hours. The first thirty minutes after your race are prime time for refueling your body, and it's very important that you do so within that time frame. Not that you can't extend beyond that time frame (I kept at it for about four days after my event), but after thirty minutes you're really just adding pounds to your body, rather than healing or refueling it (as if that were reason to stop eating).

You've probably been experimenting throughout your training with things you enjoy eating postride, so you know whether you prefer eating some food or drinking a recovery drink that is formulated to replace your lost nutrients. Stick with what you like on race day and perhaps throw in some of the food they are offering at the finish line, too.

And then, off to that party and nap.

Load Up

When I was traveling through Switzerland on a bike, I enjoyed having a handlebar bag on my bike. It's a bag that can quickly be attached to and removed from the front of a bike's handlebars, and it holds all sorts of goodies. I found it helpful to be able to load up this bag with my water, map, and camera, a spare long-sleeve shirt, and some Swiss chocolate (important cycling food). I could reach into the bag and dig out anything I needed (I found that I needed chocolate *a lot*) without having to stop riding.

I was looking forward to getting one of these nifty bags for my bike when I returned to the U.S. of A. I thought it would be a great thing to have on my century ride, since I've yet to master the act of pulling my water bottle from its holder beneath my legs without running the bike off the road and into a tree. Being able to drink regularly while I'm riding is a huge deal, and it's a pain to have to stop all the time to make sure I'm hydrating. I usually end up not stopping, and then I'm not hydrating, and then, well, I've read that bad things can happen when you don't hydrate. Things involving hospitals.

But for some reason, the handlebar bags that they have here in the U.S. of A don't fit my bike. Or I guess they could fit, if I didn't mind losing access to one set of brakes. And while I think hydrating is important, I feel like braking is pretty high up there on the cycling necessities list as well. In fact, I'd venture to guess that I brake quite a bit more than I hydrate. So the American handlebar bags are out.

The other alternative is panier bags, also referred to as saddlebags. They go on a rack that attaches to the back of

>>>

your bike, and they hang over either side of your tire. These things are common for people who are doing bike tourism and carry all of their clothes and necessities on the bike with them as they travel around. These people need to reevaluate their idea of a vacation, I'd say. Paniers are also used by bike commuters who need to bring their work stuffs with them somehow and feel like a backpack might make them look dorky.

Panier bags don't give me the direct access I had with handlebar bags, but they at least allow me to load up some necessities for my rides. (You never know when I might come across some more chocolate that I need to purchase.) I had my Bike Dude put the rack on the back of my bike, and then I put the paniers on and I was ready to roll. Unfortunately, the first time I tried out these paniers was on my second attempt at a century ride. You know how they say you should never try out something new on the day of a big event? There is a significant reason for that.

I think the size of paniers is what ultimately caused my downfall. They have the capacity to hold about four times as much stuff as my handlebar bags (chocolate in bulk!), and for some reason I felt like this meant I had to fill them. I might have gotten a little out of hand.

The night before my century, I started loading up my bags with everything a good cyclist needs: a pair of pants (for after the race), flip-flops (to get comfy after the race), a jacket (for the cold morning), my camera (to capture the moments), my journal (to capture the moments), a map, a spare tire tube, flat-tire tools, butt balm, Gatorade mix, Goo, granola bars, and some pretzels.

>>>

It seems as though I was treating my paniers sort of like someone would treat a trunk of a car in preparation for a long road trip. I was throwing anything and everything into the bags that I might need on the ride. The difference between panier bags and the trunk of a car is that you don't have to pull the trunk contents along the road with the strength of your thigh muscles (unless you are trying to be ecological and cut down on gas). Instead of thinking about those poor thigh muscles during my packing process, I was thinking things like *I really don't like the way my butt looks in these bike shorts; I better bring something to wear over them for after the race* and *I like flip-flops*. And my favorite: *I might get introspective on my ride; I should bring a journal.*

Shocker of shockers, I didn't end up getting introspective. But if I had decided to whip out the journal, I probably would have written something along the lines of "If you find this journal by the side of the road, know that it has been thrown here intentionally by a cyclist trying desperately to lighten her load. P.S. If you have any sort of rash in your nether regions, there is some Butt Balm about fifty yards up the road. Godspeed."

My Century, Take 1

I signed up for the NYC Century Bike Tour because I was looking for a century ride that was a little more entertaining than some of the ones I'd found while searching online. Most of the rides described routes that wound through miles and miles of open land. Snore. I had just returned from traveling through Europe on a bike and was ready to see even more of the world on two wheels. The thought of touring around New York sounded exciting, and exciting sounded like a great way to keep my mind off the fact that I was riding one hundred miles.

The good news is, I was right. New York definitely kept my mind off the fact that I was riding one hundred miles. Unfortunately, my mind was mostly concerned with whether I would live to see even one more mile. Whose idea was it to ride a bike in *New York City?* Hello! There are, like, *eight million* friggin' people in that city, many of whom are traveling by car or are walking very fast. This is not a place to be attempting a long-distance cycling event. And yet attempt I did—"attempt" being a very key word here.

I did the ride with my friend Ruth, who is an outstanding cyclist and a native New Yorker to boot. What more could you ask for in a sidekick for the NYC century, right? She would lead me around the city to cycling glory. It would be awesome.

Ruth and I were also joined by Sherry, who wasn't really feeling the one-hundred-mile route. She decided to head off on the fifteen-mile route and then go for cocktails while she waited for us to finish. I feel like maybe Sherry should be on the planning committee for next year's event, because

>>>

>>>

her New York ride turned out a lot better than ours. Maybe cocktails were the key to her success.

We started the day bright and early, before the sun even showed itself. Because that's what athletes do: They get up before dawn. If I could somehow find a sport that involved rising at 2:00 PM, I think I might have a much better chance at success. I'm just saying. But alas, cycling is not that sport. So rise we did, and sunny it was not.

We hopped on our bikes and rode to the start line in Central Park. And rode. And rode. The ride to the ride was a ride in itself. The fact that I was a bit tired after the ride to the ride should have been a good indicator of how the rest of the day was going to go. Once we got to the start line, we were supposed to gather with the group that was riding the same distance as we were. There were 100-, 75-, 55-, 35-, and 15-mile routes to choose from. Ruth looked at me and said, "Wanna do the 75-mile route instead?" Seventy-five miles?! We were here to tackle a century, ride to glory, challenge our minds and our bodies! "Yeah, okay," I shrugged. There would be other opportunities for a century ride—why rush into it?

So right off the bat, our race was going quite well. Poof! Twenty-five miles of our ride had disappeared. We lined up with the seventy-five-milers and waited our turn to take off. When it was time, our group took off down the streets of New York City, ready to tackle our long ride with vigor and excitement. And then we stopped about five feet later.

You see, there is something to be said for doing a bike ride somewhere with open land. Open land doesn't have stoplights every fifty yards. And New York does. If we were lucky, we'd get three or four blocks before we hit a red light and

>>>

had to stop. This did not make for the quickest of rides. We wound our way through the city, riding with cars and traffic lights. Luckily, it was pretty early in the morning, so the traffic hadn't gotten out of hand yet. But it was still pretty damn scary to be navigating our way through potholed streets and numerous erratic taxis. I had my hand permanently on my brake, ready to stop at a moment's notice. "Leisurely" was not a word I could use to describe this ride.

One of the most difficult parts of the ride was trying to get used to riding with cyclists who rode in a very aggressive way. I am not an aggressive rider. I yield to automobiles because they could kill me. But serious cyclists ride with an authority and sense of entitlement that frighten me. Their assumption that all cars are going to stop is one that I don't quite share. I'd like to believe that most drivers are aware of their surroundings and will always stop in time to avoid flattening a bike, but quite frankly, I'm not willing to risk my brain matter by hoping drivers will be competent.

My timid riding style left me trying to play catch-up a lot because I actually stopped at red lights and didn't cut in front of cars, whereas other riders just sorta went where they wanted, when they wanted. I wish I could have been braver, but I just didn't have it in me. I was way too paranoid about getting hit.

Apparently, I should have been worried about hitting someone instead. I was following a group of riders as they were trying to cross a street. The street was a little weird because there were cars merging onto the road at the same place where we were trying to cross. Most of the other riders just crossed the street, cutting in front of cars with abandon.

>>>

I was too scared to do that, so I tried to time it just right so I could fall behind a car and cut over. This plan would have worked smashingly if one of the other cyclists hadn't, at the very same time, decided to cut in front of the car I was cutting in back of. This biker scared the driver, causing her to slam on her brakes, which in turn forced me to slam on my brakes. Sadly, I didn't slam on the brakes in time and instead went slamming into the back of the car. I was able to stick out my leg and take most of the hit with my knee, so I didn't hurt her car or the bike, which I thought made the crash a relative success. I was also, after a very near failure, able to stay on the bike and not go flying over my handlebars onto the ground. So overall, the crash wasn't that bad, and it was nice to get it out of the way so early in the day.

Following my accident, we made our way to the Brooklyn Bridge. We had been riding for quite some time by this point. I hadn't been looking at the route sheet at all because (1) I was far too concerned with not being run over by a car to look at anything besides oncoming automobiles, and (2) I find it's better that I not know how far I've gone on long rides. It depresses me to know how much farther I have to go. If I have the route sheet out, I can't stop myself from looking down every four minutes to see if perhaps I've magically traveled an additional fifteen miles, and I am always sorely disappointed when I see how little ground I've covered.

I had left it up to Ruth to guide us through our route sheet, and I was looking forward to finding out how far we had gone in the previous couple of hours. I was sure we had to be at least a third, maybe even halfway, through our ride. When we stopped on the Brooklyn Bridge to take a picture, I asked

>>>

her, "Do I want to know how far we've gone?" To which she quickly replied, "No." Then she put her helmet back on and took off again. This of course made me want nothing more than to know how far we'd gone. It had to be at least twenty or thirty miles. We'd been riding for *two friggin' hours*. Anything less than twenty would be both unacceptable and alarming, considering how far we were supposed to be riding.

Once we got to Brooklyn, we stopped at a little coffee shop so that Ruth could caffeinate her brain. We sat there as she sipped coffee and I sipped Gatorade, and I asked again, "How far have we gone, really?"

"You really don't want to know."

"You have to tell me. It's gotta be at least twenty miles, right?"

"You really want to know?"

"It's bad."

"It's bad."

"Tell me."

"Seven miles."

"Haaaaaaaaaaaaaaaaaaaaaaaaaaaaaaaaaaaaaaaa." I let out one of those laughs people let out right before they get taken away in a straitjacket. A "this isn't funny at all, but I'm either going to start laughing or shoot random passersby, so I think laughing might be the better option" laugh.

How *in the hell* had we gone only seven miles? I could have *crawled* seven miles in less time. And that's not even much of an exaggeration. Yet, because we'd spent two hours riding our bikes through the busiest city in the country, we had just managed the impossible. I was now riding a bike even more slowly than I used to run. It's hard to do anything (including sleeping) more slowly than I used to run. Awesome.

After Ruth finished her coffee and I finished my mental breakdown, we hopped back on our bikes and continued on our ride. A ride that was looking like it was going to take us over twenty hours to complete. Maybe I should have eaten a muffin at the coffee shop.

Luckily, things picked up a bit as we wound through Brooklyn. The streets weren't as busy as Manhattan's, and that allowed us to go a little further between red-light stops. We were still hardly moving at an acceptable pace, but we were slowly chipping away at our miles. After a little while of this chipping, we came across an unofficial rest stop: Nathan's Famous Hot Dogs. Suddenly, this ride was starting to look up.

The lines for hot dogs were out the door at this Coney Island restaurant. I got in one anyway because a hot dog and french fries sounded like outstanding athlete fuel. How much do I love cycling? And the fact that I can stop cycling, eat a four-course meal, and start cycling again without any real stomach problems? I can't think of any other sport where that would be an option. I recently went to Mexican food four hours before I played soccer, and I spent the entire game feeling as though I might vomit all over the opposing team (which would probably be a lot more effective than my normal defensive strategy). But cycling is the only sport I've found that is conducive to binge eating *during* the activity. In fact, I think it's my favorite part of the sport, quite frankly.

I polished off a hot dog, french fries, and a lemonade, and we got back on the road. We lost a little bit of time with the hot dog stop because of the half-hour wait. Most people

>>>

would have given up, but waiting in line for french fries is just the type of endurance event I was born to complete.

Things went well for another hour or so as we finally got on some actual bike paths, free of cars and potholes. We cruised along, admiring the pretty beaches and being thankful that we weren't caught in the completely stopped traffic we could see over on the freeway. It was lovely.

And short-lived.

We turned back onto city streets and were there for only a short time before I felt something explode against my leg. I looked down, expecting that I had dropped something on the ground. Maybe one of my water bottles had fallen. I didn't see anything, so I got off the bike and backed up. There was nothing there, so I had to figure it had been nothing. I hopped back on the bike and started to pedal. Then I realized it hadn't been nothing. I looked down again and saw that my poor tire had exploded. Good times.

Ruth was way ahead of me by now, because she didn't realize I had stopped. I started pushing the bike down the street, hoping that she'd come back to me eventually. And she did, greeting me with an "oh no."

"Yeah, it exploded."

She looked down at the tire. "Well, get out your spare tube."

"My spare tube?"

"Yeah, didn't they give you a spare tube at the cycle shop?"

"Um . . . "

"You didn't ask for a spare tube?"

"Um . . . "

>>>

>>>

"That's not good."

We both started looking around randomly, as if perhaps the answer to our dilemma could be found within a two-block radius. About five seconds later, a nice man pulled up beside us on his bike, eagerly wanting to help. "Can I be of assistance, ladies?"

I pointed down to my tire. "It's flat."

"Do you have a spare tube?"

"I do not."

"Well, let's see what we can do."

Then this complete stranger laid his bike down, took a bunch of tools and patches and glue out of his pack, flipped my bike over, and went about trying to fix my flat. God bless him. He tried for a while, while Ruth tried to come up with a plan B. It seemed she didn't have much faith in our good Samaritan, "Maybe there's a bike shop near here? Or a gas station might be able to fill it up." Ruth was on the phone, dialing away, trying to find our solution.

Meanwhile, Random Helper Guy worked diligently on the tire, got it all patched and pumped, and put back on the bike. Then he flipped it over and I climbed on. It immediately went flat. And so did Random Helper Guy's face. He really wanted it to work. Probably not as much as Ruth and I did, though.

We thanked Random Helper Guy for his help, and then we pushed our bikes down to the nearest gas station, in hopes of getting a cab to take us to the nearest bike shop. We walked into the minimart of the gas station and asked the employee if he could call us a cab. The minimart guy pointed behind us to a man holding a $10 bill. "He's a cab." The $10 bill man smiled and said he would be happy to take us wherever

>>>

we needed to go. Then he saw our bikes and said that he would be happy to take one of us wherever we needed to go, and that the other one would have to ride her bike, because both bikes wouldn't fit in the car. Ruth seemed okay with this idea because the bike shop was supposed to be pretty close. I was not okay with this idea, because this is the way missing-persons reports start.

"No, we're both going in the cab with you; we'll fit both bikes in the back seat. Hers is all compact and whatnot—we'll be fine." The cabby looked at me and then at the bikes and then at his car. Then he shrugged. "We try."

We did try, and we were able to get both bikes into the back seat after much cussing and maneuvering. Ruth and I piled into the front seat, where I'm pretty sure I sat on a bible, four reggae tapes, and a hamburger wrapper, which were what remained after the cab driver cleaned up the front seat. I whispered to Ruth, "I'm not entirely sure this is a cab." She shrugged. "Well, the bikes are in here, so we might as well just go with him."

With that roaring wave of confidence in our driver and our chances of not being slaughtered, we took off toward the nearest bike shop. Which wasn't so much near as it was all the way back by the damn hot dogs. The entire ride to the bike shop, I was saying, "We just rode this, we've already been here, we are *backtracking,* I can't do these miles again."

Remember that stopped traffic on the freeway? We were now part of it. And we were a part of it that was about to run out of gas. I looked down at the gas gauge on the dashboard and saw that it read three miles until empty. I once again started one of my psychotic laughs. Turns out there was a reason our driver was standing at a gas station holding $10 when we met him. And perhaps he should have completed that transaction, because now we were three miles away from having a car with no gas and a bike with no tire. At that point, I would have completely understood had Ruth finally given up on this "all for one" idea and left me and the Jamaican cabbie to our own devices while she went and met up with Sherry for some cocktails.

Thankfully, the grand state of New York randomly has gas stations in *the middle of the freeway*. I don't know why, but there it was, so perfectly placed (it appeared just as the last mile was ticking off the gas gauge) that I thought perhaps my psychotic break had finally occurred and I was hallucinating. We waited as our cabbie hopped out and filled up. We both just rubbed our faces about the absurdity of our current situation.

Jamaican Cabbie dropped us off at the bike shop, and I went in to find that I was far from the only person requiring bike assistance this lovely afternoon. While we waited, Ruth began picking the brain of a local, trying to find us an alternate route back to Manhattan. The thought of having to retrace our steps was just not something either one of us could entertain at this point. The Bike Dudes at the shop outlined a route for Ruth that would circle around and eventually meet back up with the actual century ride we were supposed to be doing.

With a newly inflated tire and somewhat deflated enthusiasm, we took off in an unknown direction, no longer traveling anywhere near the race route. Things had taken a bizarre turn, to say the least. We rode for quite a few more miles,

>>>

winding in and out of neighborhood streets, until we finally came out somewhere in Manhattan.

Ruth pulled over and looked at her map. "We can go to the finish line of the race or we can head back to the hotel. What do you want to do?"

"They are in opposite directions?"

"Pretty much."

"How long have we been riding today?"

"We started eleven hours ago."

"I want to be done now."

"So, back to the hotel?"

"Do you think Sherry is still drinking cocktails?"

"Sherry is always drinking cocktails."

"I need to drink. A lot."

"Back to the hotel."

"Back to the hotel."

So instead of joining the rest of the riders at the finish line, we joined Sherry at the Mexican restaurant across the street from the hotel. And instead of getting a free T-shirt from the ride organizers, we got guacamole and margaritas from Sherry. I feel like we made the right choice. One of true warriors.

Our stats for the day: 11 hours, 60 miles, 2 hot dogs, 1 crash, 1 flat tire, and 1 cab ride.

My first attempt at a century ride might not be considered a rousing success. But I have never tasted a better margarita in my life, so at least something good came of it.

My Century, Take 2

Seeing as my first attempt at a century ride didn't go so well, I was forced to find another event to tackle. My first century entailed eleven hours, a flat tire, a collision with an automobile, a taxi ride, and only sixty miles actually ridden. So, needless to say, my expectations for my second attempt weren't too high. If I could avoid the aid of an automobile, I would consider the day a success.

I picked a century ride close to my home, called Foxy's Fall Century. It would start in Davis and wind its way through the Napa Valley. I was told that the Napa portion of the ride was quite hilly and difficult. In addition, I was told that the Napa portion of the ride didn't include any famous Napa wine, which I felt would go a long way in easing the pain of the hills. Despite this discouraging news, I still decided this race was for me, mostly because it was only a half hour from my house, and after riding in Europe and New York, I thought perhaps my cycling budget would be well served by an event that didn't require airfare and room service.

I stayed the night with my aunt, who lives in Davis, and still had to wake up before the sun did in order to get to the ride on time. I'm not a huge fan, nor am I capable, of doing anything that involves thinking when I get out of bed that early in the morning. Which has to be the main excuse for why I chose not to eat anything for breakfast besides a hard-boiled egg. The only possible reason I might have thought this was a good idea was that I may have been recalling my early-morning marathon training runs and the fact that I couldn't eat very much before heading out to run. It upset my

>>>

>>>

stomach and made me feel nauseous if I ate anything before I started pounding the pavement. Apparently, I was *not* thinking of the numerous croissants and eggs I had eaten before heading out on a full day of cycling in Europe. Because that was a whole different country. I was on American soil now. I don't eat before endurance events when I'm in my homeland. Brilliant.

I showed up at 7:00 AM to begin my next attempt at one hundred miles. I would be doing this ride alone, and it was the first time I'd headed out on a long ride by myself. This was a little scary, to be honest. On all my previous long rides I'd merely hopped on the bike and followed a friend in front of me, never having to worry about silly things like route sheets and miles. It was nice to just ride and ride and ride and never really know where I was or how much farther I had to go. It turns out nothing makes a distance seem long quite like knowing how long the distance is, and how much more you have left. Without someone to follow blindly, I would have to make note of where I was on the route sheet, and then I'd have to make note to cry as a result. I was not looking forward to this, although what's a long-distance event without a little crying, really? It's sort of my calling card.

I went and picked up the silly route sheet before I started the race, and I studied it as though I were going to be quizzed later. I'm not entirely sure why I were so worried about the sheet, because as it turned out there were quite a few other cyclists at this event. And on the whole, they were probably going to be following the same route I was. The only thing studying the route sheet really did was ingrain in my head exactly where the rest stops were supposed to be. As I started

>>>

>>>

the ride, I knew the first rest stop was at about mile 20, so I was looking forward to getting to that one quickly and getting an idea of what kind of time I was making.

I probably shouldn't have looked quite so forward to the first rest stop, as it took me quite some time to actually get there. Hours seemed to tick by as I pedaled along, being passed every four or five seconds by a whizzing bike. I started to feel like maybe there was something wrong. Maybe the rest stop was farther away than just twenty miles, because surely I should have gone twenty miles by now. I couldn't figure out how it was that I was pedaling so hard and just not moving all that fast. Not that I'm used to moving fast, because Lord knows "fast" isn't on my list of possible speeds, but I felt like I was going even slower than normal. Which is cause for concern, because, well, my normal speed is cause enough for concern.

After hour two of not seeing mile 20, I realized that I was having some issues. The first issue was that I was starting to feel very, very hungry. Apparently, my power breakfast of one hard-boiled egg wasn't quite meeting my fueling requirements. Once I started to feel hungry and light-headed, I pulled over and ate some of the many snacks I had in my bag. But the key to keeping yourself fueled is to not wait until you get hungry, because by then you are just playing catch-up, instead of maintaining your energy level. So now I was playing catch-up not only with 96 percent of the cyclists in the race, but also with my own digestive system.

Also, it didn't help that I had recently put those panier bags on the back of my bike, and that this was the first time I'd taken the bike for a ride with the bags all loaded up. And

>>>

when I say "all loaded up," I mean I was one roll of duct tape away from being ready for the end of days. It turns out that bikes are constructed light for a reason, that reason being that light bikes move much faster than ones weighed down by an entire cycle shop's-worth of stuff. Maybe I should have paid more attention in science class.

I finally made it to the first rest stop about two and a half hours into my ride. This was not looking good from a mathematical standpoint. I was supposed to ride one hundred miles. It had taken me two and a half hours to ride twenty miles. Which meant that it would take me twelve and a half hours to do this race. Which didn't sound like too much fun. It was 9:30 AM now, which would have me ending the race at 7:30 PM at the earliest. It would be dark then. All of this math wasn't even taking into consideration that it had taken me two and a half hours to ride on *flat* land. Who could even guess how long it would take to ride the hilly miles that were promised later on?

As I stuffed my starving belly full of every food the rest stop had to offer (peanut butter on a muffin tastes remarkably good, FYI), I started to reevaluate my goals for this particular ride. I really wanted to do a century ride and I really wanted to do one today, but I also really wanted to actually finish one today, before it was tonight and hopefully before it was tomorrow. I sat for a long time trying to figure out how I could turn this around, how I could crunch the numbers and make them work. Sadly, my cycling abilities were always going to be part of the equation, so every time, the answer was not a positive one.

>>>

I knew the race had several different routes of varying lengths. I was wearing a white wristband, so I was supposed to follow the white arrows on the ground. As I'd been riding, though, I had noticed there were green arrows on the ground as well. I knew that the green arrows would veer off eventually, leading their followers along a shorter route. I wasn't sure exactly how short that route was, but I was sure that I was going to start following the green arrows instead. This was my only hope of making it to the finish line during daylight hours. I was really disappointed, because I really wanted to do the whole one hundred miles, and it seemed sort of pointless to do anything less, because wasn't one hundred why I was out here?

But I was in the middle of nowhere and I did have to finish the race somehow, so the green arrows became my new beacon, the force that would guide me to my home—so that I could get online and try to find *another* century ride to tackle.

I rolled along on the green route for quite some time, not really knowing where I was or how far I had gone. I didn't have a route sheet for this ride, which was probably better for me because I was able to put the miles out of my mind. I didn't know exactly how many miles it was to the next rest stop, so I didn't worry too much about it.

After some time of not worrying too much, I began to worry a little. I was getting really hungry again and my back was killing me. I found a shaded spot on the side of road and pulled over to eat some of the food that I had stashed at the first rest stop. I pushed a muffin in my mouth and chewed vigorously. A little too much muffin, it would seem, because I

>>>

inhaled slightly and managed to get some of the muffin stuck in my throat. This was not good. I tried to cough it up, but I couldn't get enough of a breath to cough. Tears flooded my eyes and I thought, *I'm going to die out here on the side of a friggin' road while doing a century ride. And the last thing anyone is going to think about me is that I am not even on the one-hundred-mile route and am therefore dying a slacker.*

I'm not sure how long I nearly died for, but it seemed like forever and three days. After I tried several self-Heimlich maneuvers and flailed about wildly for quite some time, I was finally able to cough up my muffin and avoid death while wearing spandex. Thank the lord. It wouldn't have been a pretty way to go out.

About two minutes after my near-death experience, I turned a corner and came across the next rest stop. For a moment I thought perhaps I actually *had* died, because I imagine heaven would have a lunch spread comparable to the one at this rest stop. I piled a plate full of sandwiches and chips and cookies, then made my way to a nice piece of grass and stuffed my face with reckless abandon and complete lack of caution toward my still sore esophagus. Then, after my face was sufficiently stuffed, I laid back on the grass and closed my eyes, hoping to get a little relief from my throbbing back pain.

It seems as though I was the only participant who thought that a catnap was a good idea, because everyone who walked past me asked me if I was okay, seemingly afraid that my horizontal state was a sign that I needed medical attention. Eventually I got tired of responding to all these people, so I grabbed my phone and called a friend of mine. I was still horizontal, but I was also on the phone, and people in need of medical attention aren't usually able to carry on normal phone conversations.

"Colleen, I need you to talk to me so these strangers will stop being concerned about my well-being."

"What are you doing?"

"I'm doing a one-hundred-mile bike ride, and I'm lying down on the grass in the middle of the rest stop."

"Where are you?"

"I'm at some park with water and boats; I think it's called Lake Solano."

"Oh! I know where that is. Do you want me to come get you?"

"What?! No! Why would you say that?"

"You just said you're lying down in the middle of the rest stop. I thought maybe you need a ride."

"No! Don't offer me a ride. I'm horizontal right now. I'm weak."

"Okay, well, it would only take me fifteen minutes to get there, if you wanted a ride."

"Ugh, you're killing me."

"Sorry. How many miles do you have left?"

"I don't know. I went off the one-hundred-mile route a while ago, I don't know where I am or where the end is."

"Wait, you're not even doing a century? What's the point, then?"

"You have a good point. . . . "

"I'm getting my keys."

"Don't tell anyone I'm a slacker, 'kay?"

"You're passed out at the rest stop. I think they might already know."

>>>

Looks like century ride v3.0 is going to have to be the charm for me, 'cause the first two attempts did not work out so well. I promise my bike will not make its way into any automobiles during the race next time. It's important to set goals.

My Century, Take 3

After two failed attempts at riding one hundred consecutive miles on my bike, I was starting to get desperate for a century ride I could actually complete. It was late in the cycling season, so it was hard to find many options when I searched the Internet for available rides. I really didn't want to travel out of town again, so I thought it best to stay local for my next attempt. There were no organized rides near my town, so I resorted to the next best thing—a marginally organized ride. One marginally organized by me.

It didn't seem all that complicated, really. The only thing organized rides offer you is a hundred-mile route and arrows showing you where to turn. And rest stops. And support personnel. And a cool commemorative T-shirt, usually featuring a piece of food and/or an animal riding a bike. So then, other than the people, the food, and the T-shirt, I had everything I needed to plan my own ride. This was going to be easy.

I started out by trying to figure out a hundred-mile route, as that seemed to be the main goal of the day. I hopped on Mapquest and started putting in address after address, building a route that was about fifty miles so that I could go out and back for a total of one hundred miles. Instead of planning a bike-friendly route with lots of scenery and open roads, I thought up different friends and/or restaurants I wanted to visit along my ride. If the friends lived near a restaurant, even better.

When I was in Europe, the miles didn't seem as long because they were broken up by stops that included great food and drink. I figured that if I could create my century ride to include such stops, it would be much less traumatic for my mind and body. If only I could have somehow included a stop at the movie theater as well, it would have been the most perfect of days.

I contacted the friends and family that were unknowingly a part of my century-ride map. I made sure they were going to be around on the day of my ride, and that they would be available to eat food with me when I got to them. They were all more than willing to help me out with my athletic endeavors.

"No, I don't want to ride a hundred miles with you—are you crazy?" Sommer asked.

"No, *I'm* doing the hundred miles. I'm just going to stop by and see you on the way."

"Why?"

"'Cause I need to eat while I'm riding, so I thought we could go down to that sushi place by you and have a roll or two."

"While you are riding?"

"Well, I'd stop for the eating."

"And I don't have to actually ride with you, just eat?"

"Yes."

"This is my kind of event, I think."

"Perfect."

I lined up a few people in this manner, having to reassure all of them that I needed nothing besides their stomachs. Many were wary that perhaps I was going to tackle them, put a helmet on their head, and tie them onto a bike seat when I saw them. Yet they were all big enough fans of eating that they were willing to risk such an unfortunate incident.

As I started planning my ride, I got a little discouraged when I discovered that I wasn't going to be able to start at 2:00 PM, as I'd originally planned. This was my race, with my rules, and therefore I'd hoped I could start my ride after noon, instead of at a stupidly early time like all the other organized athletic events I'd done had. But then I started doing the math on how far I had to ride, how many stops I planned on making, and how early the sun was going to set, and I realized that perhaps I was going to need more than three hours to complete the task at hand. Dammit.

Since I didn't really know how long it was going to take me to actually ride one hundred miles, let alone incorporate all of my pit stops, I figured it would be better to start really early in the morning and finish way before the sun set than to be riding around the streets after dark. So, grudgingly and heartbroken, I planned to start my ride at 7:00 AM. This was beyond ridiculous, but if it was what I had to do to complete my one-hundred-mile mission, then so be it.

So, around 8:00 AM on race day, I was finally all ready and headed out on my route. The great thing about planning your own race is that the start time tends to be a *teensy* bit flexible. My route started out at my house and headed toward downtown Sacramento, where, after about ten miles of riding, I met

>>>

up with Becky for a morning hot chocolate and a muffin. Sure, I was only one-tenth of the way done, but I thought I'd reward myself with some whipped cream and carbs. So far, so good. I didn't stay with her too long because my day was young and because I had her down for a real meal later on in my route. There was no need to burn up all of our conversation topics so early in the morning. Plus, who even has conversation topics early in the morning, other than "It's early. I wish I were in bed. Discuss."

My next leg was quite long: thirty miles, all the way to Davis. I didn't set up anyone to meet me along this route because it wound through areas where no one lived and, more important, no good restaurants lived. I have family in Davis, so I knew a lovely meal awaited me upon my arrival. These miles weren't so bad, with the hopeful coolness of the morning air and all that crap. I stopped a couple times to eat some snacks I'd brought along with me. On my last century attempt, I hadn't eaten enough food before and during the race, which had left me absolutely useless as the miles wore on. Since I was tackling this ride by myself, I was trying to be extra cautious about keeping my energy levels up and my passing-out levels low. I probably overcompensated on the snacking, but feeling a little full was a lot better than feeling a little in need of an ambulance.

My ride from downtown Sacramento to Davis took me along some open roads with little traffic. I was able to make pretty good time on these roads, in part because there weren't many turns to miss, which kept me from having to look down at my route sheet for assistance. There were a couple of nice eight-mile stretches along this route that gave me a chance

>>>

>>>

to sit back, listen to my talk-radio podcasts, and zone out for a bit. I really excel at the zoning-out part of cycling.

When I got into Davis, I made my way to my aunt's house, where she had a lovely meal of pasta and bread waiting for me. She had some couches that seemed quite appealing as well. However, I was on a ride and I couldn't possibly lie down on her couches. So, after I inhaled my lunch, I simply lay down on her floor instead. While I lay there, my cousin Katy came and looked down at me. "You're only halfway done?"

"Not even halfway."

"Are you ever getting up?"

"I'm not sure."

"Might as well get it over with."

"But this is the most comfortable floor I've ever encountered."

She just shook her head and walked off, silently judging my lack of cycling prowess. Whatever. After spending much time convincing my legs, back, and ass that they really did want to finish this ride, I was finally able to sit up off of the floor. Then I promptly fell back down, in a rather dramatic display of exhaustion. No one, including the cute little dog of the house, gave me the least bit of sympathy. Without this sympathy, I was forced to sit up again. A little more time passed before my body gave in completely and was actually able to rise to my feet. Thank god I hadn't lain down on one of the couches, since there's a good possibility I would still be lying there today. When a hard floor feels like a bed of clouds and cotton, you know your body is desperate for comfort.

I shoved one more piece of french bread in my mouth and once again headed off on the open road. The kid and the cute

>>>

>>>

little dog stood on the front porch and waved me off, undoubtedly assuming that I wouldn't last another ten miles.

But last I did. The next thirty miles or so took me back to Sacramento, along the same roads I'd taken to get to Davis. A lot of open land left me plenty of time to concentrate on my aching ass. After its lovely rest, my body was none too happy to be back on this bike, spinning those pedals like crazy. All my muscles decided to voice their disapproval of this choice of activity for the entire way back to Sacramento. I stopped several times in an effort to quiet my screeching back and neck muscles, hoping that a few stretches, or simply a little time-out, would calm them down a bit. However, it seemed that stopping only gave them hope that perhaps we were done. When I climbed back on the bike, they were heartbroken all over again.

I struggled through this open terrain, counting down the miles to the sushi restaurant that awaited me at the other end of this leg. I started thinking of all the different rolls I could order, and the sauces that would be on top of them. I also started thinking of the bar that was attached to the sushi restaurant. Maybe a couple beers would do me good. Or wine. Or wine and beer? Beer has carbohydrates in it, right? It sounded like the perfect cycling drink to me. Screw Gatorade.

I was running a little behind on my schedule, so I grabbed my phone and called my friends who were meeting me at the sushi place. I told them to order with abandon and that I'd be there in about fifteen minutes. It was going to be a beautiful thing to pull up to a table full of food and beverages. Just like at an organized race, except instead of crackers and peanut butter, I was going to have raw fish and alcohol. Seriously, do I know how to plan an event or what?

>>>

>>>

After I ate my sushi and drank some of my beer (some-how it didn't taste as good as I'd imagined it would, though water tasted like heaven in liquid form), I was energized and ready to tackle the last thirty miles of my ride. Instead of nav-igating city streets for the remainder of my ride, I'd opted to hop on the local bike trail for twenty miles in an effort to do a stress-free chunk. And, well, I managed at least 50 percent of that plan. (I'll leave it up to you to guess which half I didn't quite master.) This was the first time all day I found myself rid-ing with other cyclists, so it was the first time I was reminded exactly how farkin' slowly I ride. Every single bike on the bike path zoomed past me, all of them apparently fueled by talent and vigor instead of pasta and sushi. I had to stop a few times along this stretch because my poor muscles were screaming out for relief. Thank god my aunt's couches weren't along this route, 'cause there was absolutely no way I could have avoided them. I would have just offered to reupholster them after draping my sweating body all over them.

After I was done with the longest twenty miles in the his-tory of all miles ever traveled on bike, foot, or otherwise, I lay down on a grassy area and did some serious soul-searching to gain the strength to finish the last ten miles. At this point, there really was no option besides finishing, but despite that fact, there were actually several options running through my head. I could call a cab, and no one would ever be the wiser. Of course, I'd have to kill the cab driver so he'd never tell anyone my secret. And I honestly did not have the energy for homi-cide right then, so that was out. I could call a friend and have her take me home, but I didn't have enough cash in the bank to keep her quiet, either. I could take the bus, but what the hell

>>>

>>>

do I know about taking buses? With my luck, I'd end up even farther from my house, with no option besides homicide and/ or bribery to get home.

After making quite sure that I didn't have any other pos-sibilities, I climbed back on my blasted bike and pedaled in the most pathetic fashion back to my house. As the house got closer, my legs got weaker, giving up more and more with each pedal rotation. Which seemed odd to me—did they not know how close we were to resuming our horizontal lifestyle? Why wouldn't they be energized by this? But, alas, they were not. In fact, by the time I got home, pulled into my garage, and put the bike away, the only thing I could think was *God, climb-ing the stairs to my room is gonna suck.*

And it did. But on the way to my room, I ransacked the kitchen for my postride meal I'd planned. I even turned on some music, so it was just like the finish line of a real race. Only instead of hobbling toward my car like I would have after an organized race, I hobbled toward my couch. And there I lay, pouring food and drink into my mouth while balancing ice packs on my legs and flipping through my TiVo recordings. Seriously, do I know how to plan an event or what?

Epilogue

W hen I first started out on my foray into cycling, I looked at it much as I had my previous foray into running—mostly with dread and panic. I saw it as yet another ridiculous athletic challenge that I was exposing myself to for reasons that seemed unclear as soon as my first muscle cramp kicked in. I grudgingly bought my bike and then spent months just looking at it, so hesitant was I to once again put my body through the rigors of an endurance sport. Sure, the benefits had been great—both physical and mental—when I trained for and completed a marathon, but the gain had been the result of quite a bit of pain—both physical and mental as well, coincidentally enough. It was the pain I wasn't looking forward to revisiting.

When I finally did get on my bike, I tackled cycling in the same way I'd taken on running: with a detailed schedule that laid out how far I was supposed to ride each day. I even went back to the same bike trail where I had done most of my long marathon training runs. Each day I did the miles, sweated my arse off, ate my reward carbs, and mocked how my butt looked in spandex. It all felt very familiar, if not that exciting.

Then I went through Europe. On a bike. And the world literally opened up in front of me. I rode a lot of miles every day, but somehow they were different from the ones I'd been riding back home (and I'm not just talking about the abundance of cheese and wine that marked those rides). Instead of simply heading out on a bike ride for the sole purpose of *finishing* a bike ride, I was heading out for the purpose of doing the ride, for what there was to see along the way (the wine and cheese being two of my favorite sights).

Cycling took on a completely different meaning, and suddenly I wasn't doing it just for the exercise or the challenge of it; I was doing it because it led me through some of the most gorgeous countryside I'd ever seen, into tiny villages and around huge bodies of water. Yes, I was still getting exercise and I was still being challenged, but all of a sudden those two things became secondary to cycling's other offerings.

When I returned from Europe, I continued to look at cycling in a different light. No longer was it just a chore that had to be done; it was now an adventure waiting to happen. I stopped riding exclusively on a bike trail, instead opting for rides around my neighborhood and city, ones that let me see my hometown up close and personal. I rode around New York City on a bike, on a ride that led to a flat tire, a cab ride, and several margaritas.

As I headed out on each of these rides, I began to look forward to the fact that I didn't have any idea what was going to happen (although my money was always on a flat tire; they were my calling card of sorts). I didn't know if I'd change my mind halfway through the ride and go a different route, or if I'd come across an interesting café and stop in for a quick bite (grilled-cheese sandwiches are good training food, right?). I began to see why some people consider cycling not just a sport, but rather a lifestyle. What other sport can get you to work, through the Alps, and the best parking at events?

I always go back to one of my Bike Dudes, who, when asked if he'd ever trained for a century ride, said, "Nah, we just ride, ya know?" The more I got into the sport, the more I understood what he was talking about. Sure, there are events to train for and century rides to dream of, but ultimately the real beauty of cycling can be found when you "just ride." So while I hope you are successful in any cycling endeavors you aspire to take on, most of all I hope your endeavors don't end with the completion of one event or race.

The adventures you can find while you're on the back of a bike are endless, and I hope that they are what motivate you—more than a finish line or a shrinking waistline—to hop back on your bike for years to come. Looking for fun, camaraderie, beautiful sights, physical challenges, travel, and fantastic calf muscles?

Just ride.

APPENDIX *A*

ACCESSORY CHECKLIST

Please be strong and try to stick to this list while venturing into the bike store. Remember, you don't have to buy every *single* item on your first trip to the store. If you do, you will likely send your credit card's fraud protection into a tailspin by running up a huge bill. "The closest this cardholder has ever gotten to an athletic purchase was the big-screen TV she bought in time to watch the Super Bowl—the card has obviously been stolen by a very health-conscious thief."

Have to Haves

❏ Helmet

Brains are fun. Although yours came up with the stupid idea of riding a bike for hours at a time, you should still try your best to protect it. It obviously has enough problems already.

❏ Shorts

These shorts, on the other hand, aren't fun at all. But even less fun is how your ass will feel without this apparel. Good news, though: They can also double as an adult diaper later in life. What a bargain!

Probably Should Haves

❑ Jerseys

These jerseys are designed specifically to turn you into a cycling superstar. And if that doesn't work out, the great little pouch in the back is just the right size for storing a Twinkie.

❑ Shoes

Try to find some shoes that maximize your cycling and also your postride coolness. These two criteria don't always go hand in hand with cycling shoes, so be picky.

❑ Gloves

I'm sure there are many scientific and physical reasons to have gloves. My number one reason: They'll make your inevitable first fall off your bike a little softer.

❑ Butt Butter

The name alone is reason to make the purchase.

Your Choice

❑ Glasses

Although it may appear that way, you really aren't any more aerodynamic while wearing these. But since when is appearance not enough of a reason to make a purchase?

❑ CamelBak

If you have balance like mine and are unable to grab your water bottle from your bike without veering into traffic and/or trees, a CamelBak provides a nice way to hydrate and not risk death while riding. Always a good combo.

Special Cold-Weather Attire

If you can't figure out a way to fit a space heater on your bike (and a generator, I guess), these items will prove helpful in avoiding death by frozen body parts:

- ❏ Jackets
- ❏ Arm/leg warmers
- ❏ Gloves with fingers
- ❏ Beanie/headband
- ❏ Foot warmers/booties

APPENDIX *B*

CENTURY CHECKLIST

Pack all of this stuff the night before your race, take time with it, and check things off as you put them on the pile o' fun. I've also included a few blank spaces for you to list any personal-preference stuff you may want to take on your ride. For instance, my list would include a box of wine. Look, we all have our tools—there's no need to judge.

Your Outfit

For the first time ever, you will be with a mass of people who all look as ridiculous as you do in your riding outfit. Expect to be overwhelmed by camaraderie. And perhaps a little fear.

❑ Shorts

❑ Helmet

❑ Jersey

❑ Shoes/socks

❑ Gloves

❑ Glasses

Other Stuff

❏ Butt Butter

Sometimes this is available at the event. But it is never gonna seem sanitary to use the event's offering of something with the word "Butt" in the name.

❏ CamelBak/water bottle

Or maybe one of those helmets with a can on either side and two straws going into your mouth. The point is, you're gonna need a way to get liquids into your body.

❏ Sports drinks

They'll have these at the rest stops, but your body is probably more accustomed to the kind you've had while training. (I don't think the rest-stop drinks have a shot of gin and espresso in them, so they can't really compete with your homemade concoction.)

❏ Snacks/energy bars

Do you have any idea how great a cheese pizza would taste at mile 72? See if you can fit it in the back of your jersey.

❏ Race number/safety pins

Don't assume they'll have safety pins available for you at the race—somehow, these always seem to be in short supply.

❏ Cash

That Chinese restaurant at mile 64 is gonna look awfully tempting. A few potstickers never hurt anyone.

❏ Cold-weather attire (for the beginning of the race)

Sometimes races start at the crack of friggin' dawn, so you may need some warm clothes to avoid frostbite within the first five miles.

Your Stuff

❏ _____

❏ _____

❏ _____

❏ _____

❏ _____

❏ _____

❏ _____

❏ _____

❏ _____

❏ _____

APPENDIX *C*

TRAINING LOG

Always look for trends in your training log. For example, when the quality of a workout is 1 out of 5, what was your nutrition like? How were you sleeping? Fighting a cold? What variables affect your workout and overall feeling? A training log not only allows you to see your progress, but also allows you to see when you may need a rest!

For subjective reporting of "quality" and "overall feeling," use a 1-5 scale (5 is best). Print this out each week and keep it in your training log binder.

As you train week after week, your rides and your miles and your butt aches all become a blur (except the butt aches—they actually stand out quite clearly). But as in any journey in life, it's difficult to fully deduce where you are without first knowing where you've been. I know that might be a bit deep for the training portion of this book, but go with me on this one. The first thing you are going to do is start a training log. You are going to be spending several months exposing your body to unnatural physical challenges and crotch rashes. The very least you can do is keep written proof that at one point in your life you were actually able to eat as many carbs as you wanted without fear of going up two pant sizes. In the end, these are the things that really matter.

Besides merely being proof of your athletic prowess, a training log will also provide you with other fun things, like reference points and reminders, helping you to recall many of the training days you may have blocked out in a fit of post-traumatic stress.

So basically, whatever your reason for keeping a training log, you're gonna want to be thorough.

As Coach Mike says, "Always look for trends in your training log. For example, when the quality of a workout is 1 out of 5, what was your nutrition like? How were you sleeping? Fighting a cold? What variables affect your workout and overall feeling? A training log not only allows you to see your progress, but also allows you to see when you may need a rest!"

Training Log

Monday	Tuesday	Wednesday	Thursday
DATE	DATE	DATE	DATE
OVERALL FEELING	OVERALL FEELING	OVERALL FEELING	OVERALL FEELING
SLEEP QUALITY	SLEEP QUALITY	SLEEP QUALITY	SLEEP QUALITY
BREAKFAST	BREAKFAST	BREAKFAST	BREAKFAST
SNACK	SNACK	SNACK	SNACK
LUNCH	LUNCH	LUNCH	LUNCH
SNACK	SNACK	SNACK	SNACK
DINNER	DINNER	DINNER	DINNER
TODAY'S WORKOUT	TODAY'S WORKOUT	TODAY'S WORKOUT	TODAY'S WORKOUT
WORKOUT QUALITY	WORKOUT QUALITY	WORKOUT QUALITY	WORKOUT QUALITY
TOMORROW'S PLAN	TOMORROW'S PLAN	TOMORROW'S PLAN	TOMORROW'S PLAN

Training Log

Friday	Saturday	Sunday
DATE	DATE	DATE
OVERALL FEELING	OVERALL FEELING	OVERALL FEELING
SLEEP QUALITY	SLEEP QUALITY	SLEEP QUALITY
BREAKFAST	BREAKFAST	BREAKFAST
SNACK	SNACK	SNACK
LUNCH	LUNCH	LUNCH
SNACK	SNACK	SNACK
DINNER	DINNER	DINNER
TODAY'S WORKOUT	TODAY'S WORKOUT	TODAY'S WORKOUT
WORKOUT QUALITY	WORKOUT QUALITY	WORKOUT QUALITY
TOMORROW'S PLAN	TOMORROW'S PLAN	TOMORROW'S PLAN

Acknowledgments

D iving into the world of cycling was a daunting task, one that would have been impossible if not for the help and patience of the many family members, friends, and complete strangers who offered their support, knowledge, and general mockery throughout the training for and writing of this book.

To Jodi Holmes, Rebekah Rook, Rachel Wanner, Heather Webster, Jay Wester, Mo Mata, Travis Henderson, Sarah Smith, Roz Bostock, Cuba, Sarah Bradley-Gibson, Sommer Wilson, Todd Lampe, Michaela Borris, Erika Marsh, Vince Jacob, Lauren Weston, Colleen Scotten, Elisa Rivera, and everyone else who put up with me during the course working on this book. The fact that none of you beat me over the head with a bike lock says quite a bit about your dedication to our friendship.

To Karen Cooper, Hannah Hurley, Kellan London, David Gossett, Jodi Holmes, Andrea LaMattina, Ruth Romer, Howard Barsky, Dena Ringold, Amber Nelson, The Bike Dudes at Natomas Bike Shop, and the many Random Cyclist People who took the time to help me along the way to cycling glory (and more important, cycling knowledge). It never fails to amaze me how willing people are to help out complete idiots who come barreling into their beloved sport with nothing more than sarcasm and low pain thresholds.

To Sherry Stewart and Edwin Abele, as well as countless other people throughout the land who helped me execute a cross-country road trip to promote my first book. Without their transportation, support, and humor *NonRunner's* wouldn't have reached nearly as many people, and without that success *NonCyclist's* wouldn't have been possible.

To Katy and Rose Marie, for their love and support, and weekly home-cooked meals.

To my parents, Betty Lou and Dave Dais, who still roll their eyes when I get crazy ideas, but never stop believing that I can actually make them happen.

To my agent, Lilly Ghahremani, for always getting my back.

And lastly, to Brooke Warner, my editor on this book and the last. Her encouragement and patience throughout the (very slow) writing of this book kept me going when all I really wanted to do was hurl my computer and all things cycling-related off a very tall bridge. If it weren't for her (and my lack of upper body strength) this book would still be nothing more than a few notes scribbled on my palm ("Cyling. Ouch.") while I was passed out at an event rest stop.

Thank you.

About the Author

© DAN HOOD

Dawn Dais has always taken great pride in her ability to expend the minimum amount of calories necessary to accomplish all things in life. She finds it beyond ironic and quite troubling that her two books, *The NonRunner's Marathon Guide for Women* and *The NonCyclist's Guide to the Century and Other Road Races,* involve nothing short of calorie-burning bonanzas. When she is not exposing her poor muscles to pain and agony for the sake of her art, she can be found lounging peacefully in front of her computer, doing freelance writing and graphic design work. She lives in Sacramento, California, in a small condo that is not nearly big enough for the number of animals that live there with her.

Selected Titles from Seal Press

FOR MORE THAN THIRTY YEARS, SEAL PRESS HAS PUBLISHED GROUNDBREAKING BOOKS. BY WOMEN. FOR WOMEN.

VISIT OUR WEBSITE AT: WWW.SEALPRESS.COM

The Nonrunner's Marathon Guide for Women: Get Off Your Butt and On with Your Training, by Dawn Dais. $14.95, 1-58005-205-3. Cheer on your inner runner with this accessible, funny, and practical guide.

The List: 100 Ways to Shake Up Your Life, by Gail Belsky. $15.95, 1-58005-256-8. Get a tattoo, ride in a fire truck, or use food as foreplay—this collection of 100 ideas will inspire women to shake things up and do something they never dared to consider.

The Bigger, The Better, The Tighter the Sweater: 21 Funny Women on Beauty, Body Image, and Other Hazards if Being Female, edited by Samantha Schoech and Lisa Taggart. $14.95, 1-58005-210-X. A refreshingly honest and funny collection of essays on how women view their bodies.

No Touch Monkey!: And Other Travel Lessons Learned Too Late, by Ayun Halliday. $14.95, 1-58005-097-2. A self-admittedly bumbling vacationer, Halliday shares—with razor-sharp wit and to hilarious effect—the travel stories most are too self-conscious to tell.

Dirty Sugar Cookies: Culinary Observations, Questionable Taste, by Ayun Halliday. $14.95, 1-58005-150-2. Ayun Halliday is back with comical and unpredictable essays about her disastrous track record in the kitchen and her culinary observations.

Half-Assed: A Weight-Loss Memoir, by Jennette Fulda. $15.95, 1-58005-233-9. Pastaqueen.com blogger Jennette Fulda's satisfyingly inspirational memoir about the challenges and triumphs of losing half of her 372 pounds.